THIS BOOK
BELONGS TO:

_____

The
Holy Qur'an
For Kids Juz 'Amma

A Textbook for School Children

Juz 'Amma
English / Arabic
Surahs 78-114

Presented by Yahiya Emerick

With illustrations by Patricia Meehan

To reorder go to: www.amirahpublishing.com

ISBN: 1463783272
EAN-13: 978-1463783273

Bismillahir Rahmanir Rahim

In the Name of Allah,
The Caring and the Merciful.

The Holy Qur'an for Kids – Juz 'Amma

Textbook with English *and* Arabic Text
(Treat the Book with Respect)

Reading for Comprehension.
Textbooks for Today and Tomorrow.
The Islamic Arts Series

Grade Range 3-5

By Yahiya Emerick

Illustrated by Patricia Meehan

Reading for Comprehension: Textbooks for Today and Tomorrow, is a new effort to present information on Muslims and Islam in a manner which is in keeping with current educational standards.

This simplified learning text for young children is meant to be a supplementary teaching text for use in a lower elementary classroom. The teacher is encouraged to use this text as the basis for lessons on Islam and life in general. See our website at www.amirahpublishing.com for more educational resources.

6

Juz 'Amma Chapter List

"The Two Chapters of Protection"

Dear Children...

The Qur'an is the best book to read in all the world. What makes it so special is that it is a message from the One Who made the universe and everything in it.

Imagine that! Allah cares about us so much that He gave us a guidebook to help us be the best people that we can be.

Allah sent messages like this to many prophets in the old days, but people back then lost their messages or mixed them up with old legends. That's why Allah sent more and more messages again and again.

The last person to get a message from Allah was Prophet Muhammad, peace be upon him. This message is called the Qur'an.

Allah wants us to be good people and to stay away from things that will hurt us. He uses the words of the Qur'an to teach us right from wrong and to give us the good news of a beautiful world waiting for us in the Next Life.

Allah has offered a special deal to all of us: if we are good believers here in this life, then He will save us from a scary place called Hellfire and give us happiness forever in *Jennah!*

When we read the Qur'an in the Arabic language, it makes our hearts feel good and we connect with the original words spoken to the Prophet Muhammad.

We should all learn how to read the Arabic Qur'an to get special rewards and blessings.

If we do not know what the Arabic words mean, then we can read books like this one that tell you what the Qur'an is saying.

This book offers the message of part 30 of the Qur'an in an easy to understand way.

When you get older, you can move up to the grown-up Qur'an and read the whole thing.

Try to read a little bit of the Qur'an every day. It's good for you.

The Prophet Muhammad said that a heart that ignores the Qur'an is like an empty house. When we read the Qur'an the angels come close and ask Allah to help us and give us blessings.

Make your heart a place filled with light and you will be satisfied in this world no matter what happens to you, good or bad. Then in the Next Life you can live in total happiness forever.

But don't keep the good news of Allah only to yourself. The Prophet Muhammad said that the best people are the ones who learn the Qur'an and teach it with others.

So don't be afraid to share what you have learned. Bring the light of Allah's Good Book to all the world, and then Allah has promised that He will give you an extra special reward in *Jennah!* Ameen!

Yahiya Emerick
New York
August 2011 (Ramadan!)

This is What Allah Said to His Prophet...

(Part 30 of the Holy Qur'an)

The Prophecy

78 An-Naba'
Early Meccan Period

In the Name of Allah,
the Compassionate, the Merciful

What are they arguing about? It's about the big news (of life after death), and it makes them argue *even more*. Oh no, but they'll soon know, and then, oh no, they'll soon know! [1-5]

Didn't We spread the earth out far and wide and make it secure with strong mountains? *Didn't We* create all you *people* in **pairs** (*of male and female*)? [6-8]

Didn't We give you sleep as your way to rest? *Didn't We* make the night for hiding things and the day for working? [9-11]

13

(Didn't We) build the seven skies high above you and place (the sun to be like a) burning **lamp** way up there? (Don't We) make the heavy rains fall from the clouds to grow grains, vegetables and green gardens? [12-16]

For sure, the Day of Sorting (*good people from bad people*) is at a set time. That day the horn will be blown, and you will come forward in huge crowds. The sky will open wide like it was full of doors, and the mountains will shift and vanish like a mirage. [17-20]

Hellfire will be ready to jump out (*at the bad people*), because it's the final home of the people who didn't follow (*the rules*). [21-22]

(*The bad people*) are going to stay in there for a long, long time. They won't have anything that is nice and cool nor anything to drink if they're thirsty - *except for boiling mud and stinging frost!* [23-25]

That's the payback they should get, because they never expected to be called to answer *for what they did*, and they said Our (*revealed*) verses were false. [26-28]

Oh, but We wrote down everything *they did* in a special **notebook**! [29]

So *they will be told:* "*Suffer the results of what you did! You'll get nothing more from your life except for more and more punishment!*" [30]

But those who were careful (*about their duty to Allah*) will have their greatest wish: special gardens and vineyards, wonderful companions of the same age, every cup filled to overflowing, and no more useless talk or lies to be heard. [31-35]

All this will be a **reward** from your Lord. That's an excellent payback from the Lord of the heavens, the earth and everything in between – *He is* the One Who Cares!

No one will dare argue (with *Allah*) on the day when the Spirit (*of Angel Jibra'il*) and the *other* angels line up in rows, and no one will say anything but those whom the Caring One allows to speak, and even then only the truth will be spoken. [36-38]

That will be the day of total truth. So whoever chooses, let him take the path that leads straight back to his Lord. Truly, We have warned you about a penalty that is very close.

That is the day when every person will be the witness over all the deeds that his hands have sent ahead of him (*into the next life*).

Then the one who denied *the truth* will cry, "*I'm doomed! If only I could turn into a bunch of dust!*" [39-40]

☁ Think About It

1. Why did the Arabs of Mecca argue so much about Islam?

2. Why do you think that Allah mentions wonderful things from nature in verses 6-16? What is He trying to remind people about?

3. Here is a challenge: take out a notebook and write down everything you do, think or say for the next two minutes. Can you imagine how long the angels' notebook is on you?

   Now if you were an angel writing down all the deeds that a person like you was doing, what would you think about that person?

Fill in the Words on the lines below.
Look at the **BOLD** words in the main text to see where they go

Words to Use

Pairs   Reward   Notebook   Lamp

---

1. Oh, but We wrote down everything *they did* in a special _____!

2. (Didn't We) build the seven skies high above you and place (the sun to be like a) burning _____ way up there?

3. *Didn't We* create all you *people* in _____ (*of male and female*)?

4. *All this* will be a _____ from your Lord.

بِسْمِ اللهِ الرَّحْمٰنِ الرَّحِيْمِ

عَمَّ يَتَسَآءَلُوْنَ ۟١

عَنِ النَّبَاِ الْعَظِيْمِ ۟٢

الَّذِيْ هُمْ فِيْهِ مُخْتَلِفُوْنَ ۟٣

كَلَّا سَيَعْلَمُوْنَ ۟٤

ثُمَّ كَلَّا سَيَعْلَمُوْنَ ۟٥

اَلَمْ نَجْعَلِ الْاَرْضَ مِهٰدًا ۟٦

وَّالْجِبَالَ اَوْتَادًا ۟٧

وَّخَلَقْنٰكُمْ اَزْوَاجًا ۟٨

وَّجَعَلْنَا نَوْمَكُمْ سُبَاتًا ۟٩

وَّجَعَلْنَا الَّيْلَ لِبَاسًا ۙ ﴿١۰﴾

وَّجَعَلْنَا النَّهَارَ مَعَاشًا ۪ ﴿١۱﴾

وَّبَنَيْنَا فَوْقَكُمْ سَبْعًا شِدَادًا ۙ ﴿١۲﴾

وَّجَعَلْنَا سِرَاجًا وَّهَّاجًا ۪ ﴿١۳﴾

وَّاَنْزَلْنَا مِنَ الْمُعْصِرٰتِ مَآءً ثَجَّاجًا ۙ ﴿١٤﴾

لِّنُخْرِجَ بِهٖ حَبًّا وَّنَبَاتًا ۙ ﴿١۵﴾

وَّجَنّٰتٍ اَلْفَافًا ؕ ﴿١۷﴾

اِنَّ يَوْمَ الْفَصْلِ كَانَ مِيْقَاتًا ۙ ﴿١٤﴾

يَّوْمَ يُنْفَخُ فِي الصُّوْرِ فَتَاْتُوْنَ اَفْوَاجًا ۙ ﴿١۸﴾

وَّفُتِحَتِ السَّمَآءُ فَكَانَتْ اَبْوَابًا ۙ ﴿١۹﴾

وَّسُيِّرَتِ الْجِبَالُ فَكَانَتْ سَرَابًا ؕ ﴿۲۰﴾

إِنَّ جَهَنَّمَ كَانَتْ مِرْصَادًا ۝

لِّلطَّاغِيْنَ مَاٰبًا ۝

لّٰبِثِيْنَ فِيْهَاۤ اَحْقَابًا ۝

لَّا يَذُوْقُوْنَ فِيْهَا بَرْدًا وَّلَا شَرَابًا ۝

اِلَّا حَمِيْمًا وَّغَسَّاقًا ۝

جَزَآءً وِّفَاقًا ۝

اِنَّهُمْ كَانُوْا لَا يَرْجُوْنَ حِسَابًا ۝

وَّكَذَّبُوْا بِاٰيٰتِنَا كِذَّابًا ۝

وَكُلَّ شَيْءٍ اَحْصَيْنٰهُ كِتٰبًا ۝

فَذُوْقُوْا فَلَنْ نَّزِيْدَكُمْ اِلَّا عَذَابًا ۝

إِنَّ لِلْمُتَّقِينَ مَفَازًا ۝

حَدَآئِقَ وَأَعْنَابًا ۝

وَّكَوَاعِبَ أَتْرَابًا ۝

وَّكَأْسًا دِهَاقًا ۝

لَّا يَسْمَعُونَ فِيهَا لَغْوًا وَّلَا كِذَّابًا ۝

جَزَآءً مِّن رَّبِّكَ عَطَآءً حِسَابًا ۝

رَّبِّ السَّمٰوٰتِ وَالْأَرْضِ وَمَا بَيْنَهُمَا الرَّحْمٰنِ

لَا يَمْلِكُونَ مِنْهُ خِطَابًا ۝

يَوْمَ يَقُومُ الرُّوحُ وَالْمَلٰئِكَةُ صَفًّا ۖ لَّا يَتَكَلَّمُونَ

إِلَّا مَنْ أَذِنَ لَهُ الرَّحْمٰنُ وَقَالَ صَوَابًا ۝

ذٰلِكَ الْيَوْمُ الْحَقُّ ۖ فَمَن شَآءَ اتَّخَذَ إِلٰى رَبِّهِ مَآبًا ۝

إِنَّا أَنذَرْنٰكُمْ عَذَابًا قَرِيبًا ۙ يَوْمَ يَنظُرُ الْمَرْءُ مَا قَدَّمَتْ
يَدَاهُ وَيَقُولُ الْكَافِرُ يٰلَيْتَنِي كُنتُ تُرٰبًا ۝

Surah 78 Transliteration

Bismillahir Rahmanir Rahim

1. 'Amma yatasaa-a loon?

2. 'Annin naba-il 'owdheem.

3. Alladhee hoom fee he mukh talefoon.

4. Kallaa saya' lamoon.

5. Thoomma kallaa saya' lamoon.

6. A lam naj 'alil -arda mehaada.

7. Wal jibaala owtaada.

8. Wa Khalaq naakum azwaaja.

9. Wa ja'alnaa nouw makum subaata.

10. Wa ja'al naal layla lebaasa.

11. Wa ja'alnaan nahara ma 'aasha.

12. Wa banaiynaa fow qakum sab'an she daada.

13. Wa ja'alnaa siraajan wah haaja.

14. Wa anzalna minal mu'siraati maa-an thaj jaa jaa.

15. Lee nukh reja behe habban wa nabaata.

16. Wa jannaatin al faafa.

17. Inna yowmal fasli kaana meqawta.

18. Yowma yoon fakhu fis soori fata-toona afwaaja.

19. Wa futihatis samaa-u fakaanat abwaaba.

20. Wa soo yera til jibaalu fakaanat saraaba.

21. Inna jahannama kaanat mirsawda.

22. Lit tawgheena ma aaba.

23. Laa bethena feehaa ah-qawba.

24. La yadhu qoona fee haa bardan wa laa sharaaba.

25. Illaa hamee man wa ghasaaqaw.

26. Jaza-ow we faaqaw.

27. Innahum kaanoo laa yarjoona hesaaba.

28. Wa kadh dhaaboo be ayaatinaa kidh dhaaba.

29. Wa kulla shay-in ah-saiynaahu kitaaba.

30. Fadhooqoo falan nazeedakum illaa 'adhaaba.

31. Inna lil muttaqeena mafaaza.

32. Hadaa-iqa wa 'a naaba.

33. Wa kawaa 'eba at raaba.

34. Wa ka-san dehaaqaw.

35. Laa yasma'oona feehaa laghwan wa laa keedh dhaaba.

36. Jazaa-an mir rabbeka 'ataaw-an hesaaba.

37. Rabbis samawaate wal -ardi wa maa baiyna hoomar rahmaani laa yamlee koona minhu khetawba.

38. Yowma yaqoom ur roohoo wal malaa-ikatu saffan laa yatakal lamoona illaa man adhena lahur rahmaanu wa qawla sawaaba.

39. Dhaalikal yowmul haqq. Faman sha-at takhadha elaa rabbihe ma aaba.

40. Innaa an dhar naakum 'adhaaban qareebaiy yowma yan dhoorul mar-u maa qaddamat yadaahu wa yaqoolul kaafiru ya laiytanee kuntoo turaaba.

Those Who Pull Roughly

79 An-Nāzi'āt
Early Meccan Period

🔍 BACKGROUND

This chapter was revealed immediately after surah 78 and it continues to talk about the importance of being good and why it's important to us on Judgment Day. The story of Pharaoh and how he rejected Musa (Moses) plays an important part in this section.

In the Name of Allah,
the Compassionate, the Merciful

By those *horse riders* who pull roughly *on the reins*, and those who gently loosen, by those who ride along smoothly, then pass (each other) racing, and so bring about the final result.

(From these signs think about the truth of) the day when violent shaking will strike (the earth) over and over. On that day *peoples'* **hearts** will be racing, and eyes will be downcast. [1-9]

Yet, (some people) ask, *"Huh? Are we really going to be brought back as good as new? Even after our bones have rotted away? Coming back like that would be a total waste!"*

Oh, but when a single cry goes out, they'll suddenly *be standing* wide-awake (on a big empty plain)! [10-14]

Musa and the Pharaoh

Have you ever heard the story of Musa? His Lord called out to him in the valley of Tuwa, saying:

"*Go to Pharaoh for he's out of control. Say to him, 'Would you like to clean your soul (and get rid of all your bad deeds)? I will guide you to your Lord so you can worship Him.'*" [15-19]

(And so Musa went to Pharaoh) and showed him the great sign (of Allah's power), [but he denied it and disobeyed and harshly turned his back away. [20-22]

(Pharaoh) assembled (his court) and made an announcement (to all his people). He said, "*It is I who am your supreme lord!*"

Then Allah took hold of him and made an **example** of him in the next life, as well as in the first. There's an important lesson in this for those who fear (displeasing their Lord). [23-26]

Are you harder to create than the sky He built? He raised its canopy high in the correct measurements and balanced it perfectly. He made its night hard to see and its day to show things clearly.

He molded the earth like an egg after that, and then brought out its waters and plains. He also made is steady with strong **mountains**, all this was done for you and your farm animals. [27-33]

So when the big event comes to pass, that day the human being will remember clearly what he worked for. Then the raging blaze *of Hellfire* will be presented for all to see.

Whoever went beyond the bounds (of what was good and right), and who preferred the life of this world, then he'll make his home in the raging blaze.

On the other hand, whoever feared standing in the presence of his Lord, and who controlled his desires, he'll make the Garden his home. [34-41]

(And now, Muhammad,) they're asking you about the hour: "*When will it come to pass?*" Why would you (need to) remind us about it? Your Lord has fixed the deadline.

Your **job** is only to warn those who fear (its coming). When they see that the day is finally upon them, (it will seem) as if they lived but a single night and at most until the dawn! [42-46]

💭 Think About It

1. How does Allah use the image of charging horse riders to make us better understand the rush of Judgment Day?

2. Why do you think the Pharaoh rejected Musa and the message he brought?

3. The earth is made of many layers. There is the crust, or outer shell, the mantle, or inner rock, and the yellow area at the center called the magma. How is this like an egg?

4. Choose one of the two qualities of a believer mentioned in verses 34-41. Which one do you think is harder for people to practice, and how can they get better at it?

Fill in the Words on the lines below. Look at the **BOLD** words in the main text to see where they go
Words to Use
Hearts   Mountains   Job   Example

1. He also made is steady with strong _____, all this was done for you and your farm animals.

2. Then Allah took hold of him and made an _____ of him in the next life, as well as in the first.

3. Your _____ is only to warn those who fear (its coming).

4. On that day *peoples'* _____ will be racing, and eyes will be downcast.

بِسْمِ اللهِ الرَّحْمٰنِ الرَّحِيْمِ

وَالنّٰزِعٰتِ غَرْقًا ۝١

وَّالنّٰشِطٰتِ نَشْطًا ۝٢

وَّالسّٰبِحٰتِ سَبْحًا ۝٣

فَالسّٰبِقٰتِ سَبْقًا ۝٤

فَالْمُدَبِّرٰتِ اَمْرًا ۝٥

يَوْمَ تَرْجُفُ الرَّاجِفَةُ ۝٦

تَتْبَعُهَا الرَّادِفَةُ ۝٧

قُلُوْبٌ يَّوْمَئِذٍ وَّاجِفَةٌ ۝٨

اَبْصَارُهَا خَاشِعَةٌ ۝٩

يَقُوْلُوْنَ ءَاِنَّا لَمَرْدُوْدُوْنَ فِي الْحَافِرَةِ ۝١٠

ءَاِذَا كُنَّا عِظَامًا نَّخِرَةً ۝١١

قَالُوا تِلْكَ إِذًا كَرَّةٌ خَاسِرَةٌ ۝

فَإِنَّمَا هِيَ زَجْرَةٌ وَّاحِدَةٌ ۝

فَإِذَا هُمْ بِالسَّاهِرَةِ ۝

هَلْ أَتَاكَ حَدِيثُ مُوسَى ۝

إِذْ نَادَاهُ رَبُّهُ بِالْوَادِ الْمُقَدَّسِ طُوًى ۝

اِذْهَبْ إِلَى فِرْعَوْنَ إِنَّهُ طَغَى ۝

فَقُلْ هَلْ لَّكَ إِلَى أَنْ تَزَكَّى ۝

وَأَهْدِيَكَ إِلَى رَبِّكَ فَتَخْشَى ۝

فَأَرَاهُ الْآيَةَ الْكُبْرَى ۝

فَكَذَّبَ وَعَصٰى ۞

ثُمَّ اَدْبَرَ يَسْعٰى ۞

فَحَشَرَ فَنَادٰى ۞

فَقَالَ اَنَا رَبُّكُمُ الْاَعْلٰى ۞

فَاَخَذَهُ اللّٰهُ نَكَالَ الْاٰخِرَةِ وَالْاُوْلٰى ۞

اِنَّ فِيْ ذٰلِكَ لَعِبْرَةً لِّمَنْ يَّخْشٰى ۞

ءَاَنْتُمْ اَشَدُّ خَلْقًا اَمِ السَّمَآءُ ۚ بَنٰهَا ۞

رَفَعَ سَمْكَهَا فَسَوّٰىهَا ۞

وَاَغْطَشَ لَيْلَهَا وَاَخْرَجَ ضُحٰىهَا ۞

وَالْاَرْضَ بَعْدَ ذٰلِكَ دَحٰىهَا ۞

اَخْرَجَ مِنْهَا مَآءَهَا وَمَرْعٰىهَا ۞

وَالْجِبَالَ اَرْسٰىهَا ۞

مَتَاعًا لَّكُمْ وَلِاَنْعَامِكُمْ ۞

30

فَإِذَا جَاءَتِ الطَّآمَّةُ الْكُبْرَىٰ ۞

يَوْمَ يَتَذَكَّرُ الْإِنْسَانُ مَا سَعَىٰ ۞

وَبُرِّزَتِ الْجَحِيمُ لِمَنْ يَّرَىٰ ۞

فَأَمَّا مَنْ طَغَىٰ ۞

وَآثَرَ الْحَيَوٰةَ الدُّنْيَا ۞

فَإِنَّ الْجَحِيمَ هِيَ الْمَأْوَىٰ ۞

وَاَمَّا مَنْ خَافَ مَقَامَ رَبِّهٖ وَنَهَى النَّفْسَ عَنِ الْهَوٰى ۞

فَاِنَّ الْجَنَّةَ هِيَ الْمَاْوٰى ۞

يَسْـَٔلُوْنَكَ عَنِ السَّاعَةِ اَيَّانَ مُرْسٰىهَا ۞

فِيْمَ اَنْتَ مِنْ ذِكْرٰىهَا ۞

اِلٰى رَبِّكَ مُنْتَهٰىهَا ۞

اِنَّمَاۤ اَنْتَ مُنْذِرُ مَنْ يَّخْشٰىهَا ۞

كَاَنَّهُمْ يَوْمَ يَرَوْنَهَا لَمْ يَلْبَثُوْۤا اِلَّا عَشِيَّةً اَوْ ضُحٰىهَا ۞

Surah 79 Transliteration

Bismillahir Rahmanir Rahim

1. Wan naazi'aati gharqaw.

2. Wan nashitawti nashtaw.

3. Was saabihaati sab ha.

4. Fas saabiqawti sab qaw.

5. Fal mudab biraati amra.

6. Yowma tarju foor raajefah.

7. Tat ba'oohar raadefa.

8. Qulooboey yowma -edhin waajifah.

9. Absaaruhaa khawshe'ah.

10. Yaqooloona a-innaa lamar doodoona fil haafirah.

11. -A -edhaa kunnaa 'idhawman nakhirah.

12. Qawloo tilka edhan karratun khaw sirah.

13. Fa innamaa heya zaj ratun waahedah.

14. Fa edha hoom bis saahirah.

15. Hal ataaka hadeethu Musaa?

16. Idh naadaahu rabbuhu bil wadil muqad dasi Tuwa.

17. Idh hab elaa fir'aowna innahu taghaw.

18. Fa qul hal laka elaa an tazak kaa?

19. Wa ah diyaka elaa rabbika fa takh shaa?

20. Fa arahul aayatal kubraa.

21. Fa kadh dhaba wa 'asaa.

22. Thoomma ad bara yas'aa.

23. Fahashara fa naadaa.

24. Fa qawla anaa rabbukum ul a'laa.

25. Fa akhadhahul lahu nakaalal aakhirati wal oola.

26. Inna fee dhaalika la 'ibratal lemaiy yakhshaa.

27. A- antoom ashad du khalqan amis samaa-u banaaha?

28. Rafa'a samkahaa fasawwaahaa.

29. Wa agh tasha laylahaa wa akhraja doohaahaa.

30. Wal -arda ba'da dhaalika dahaahaa.

31. Akhraja minhaa maa-ahaa wa mar'aahaa.

32. Wal jibaala arsaahaa.

33. Mataa 'al lakoom walee an 'aamekum.

34. Fa edhaa jaa-a-tit taawm matul kubraa.

35. Yowma yata dhak karul insaanu maa sa'aa.

36. Wa burrizatil jaheemu lemaiy yaraa.

37. Fa ammaa man taghaw.

38. Wa aatharal hayaatad doonya.

39. Fa innal jaheema heyal ma-waa.

40. Wa ammaa man khawfa maqawma rabbihe wa nahan nafsa 'anil hawaa.

41. Fa innal jannata heyal ma-waa.

42. Yas-aloo naka 'anis saa'ati ayyana mursaahaa?

43. Feema anta min dhikraahaa.

44. Elaa rabbeka moonta haahaa.

45. Innamaa anta mundhiru maiy yakh shaahaa.

46. Ka anna hoom yowma yar rownahaa lam yalbathoo illaa asheyatan ow duhaahaa.

He Frowned

80 'Abasa
Early Meccan Period

🔍 BACKGROUND

The Prophet was talking to some chiefs of the Quraysh tribe when a blind man named Ibn Um Maktoum came along asking to speak with him. The Prophet had been trying hard to convince these important men about Islam, so when he was interrupted, he became annoyed and frowned at the old man.

This chapter was revealed to tell the Prophet that he should not give his attention to people based on how important they were. His job was to be a teacher, and that means he has to treat everyone equally. After this chapter came to him, the Prophet was always particularly nice to Ibn Um Maktoum.

*In the Name of Allah,
the Compassionate, the Merciful*

(Muhammad) frowned and turned away * when the blind man came (and interrupted his preaching). [1-2]

But for all you knew he could've grown in **goodness** * or received a useful reminder. [3-4]

The one who thought he needed nothing * was the one to whom you gave your full attention, * though he wasn't your responsibility. [5-7]

So the one who came to you eagerly (in search of knowledge), * and who feared (Allah), * you neglected. [8-10]

Let it not be so!   This (revelation) is a **reminder** * for anyone who desires to remember (the truth). [11-12]

It's written on honored pages, * exalted and holy, * by the hands of scribes, * both noble and fair. [13-16]

Doomed to destruction is the human being! How thankless is he! * What did (Allah) create him from? - * from a little drop!

He shaped (his inner qualities), * and then made his path easy (into the world at birth).   [17-20]

Then He makes him die (one day), and then he's buried - * only to be raised up again when (Allah) wants! [21-22]

But no! How often does he fail to achieve the standards that (Allah) set for him! [23]

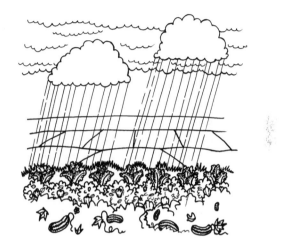

So let people **observe** the (wonders) of their food (chain). * We cause lots of rain to fall * and (make the plants) crack the dirt aside (as they grow).   [24-26]

And thus, We produce the grains, * grapes, herbs, * olives and dates. [27-29]

(We also) bring forth orchards, * fruits and grasslands, * both for you and the livestock you raise. [30-32]

Results on the Day of Judgment

🔍 BACKGROUND

A'ishah was a wife of the Prophet. She asked hom one day, "Are we all going to be judged while we're *naked?*"

The Prophet said, "Yes."

A'ishah became alarmed and said, "But that will be so embarrassing."

Then verses 33-42 were revealed explaining that no one will have any thought to notice anything except their own troubles. (Asbab ul-Nuzul)

When there comes the piercing cry * (signaling the Last) Day, a man will run from his own brother, * mother, father, * spouse and children, * for each will have concern enough for himself that day. [33-37]

Some faces will be bright on that day, * laughing and happy (for the good news they received), * while other faces will be darkened that day, * overcast (in shame). * They're the ones who **rejected** (faith) and who were disobedient. [38-42]

Think About It

1. Look at verses 1-12. What reason did Allah give for why we should not turn away from the poor and handicapped people?

2. What does this tell us about what Islam considers to be truly important in life?

3. Choose something from nature that you are most fascinated by. What is it, and how does it demonstrate that life and universe are not an accident?

4. Why do you think people will run away from each other on Judgment Day?

Fill in the Words on the lines below.
Look at the **BOLD** words in the main text to see where they go

Words to Use

Goodness   Reminder   Observe   Rejected

---

1. This (revelation) is a _____ for anyone who desires to remember (the truth).

2. So let people _____ the (wonders) of their food (chain).

3. They're the ones who _____ (faith) and who were disobedient.

4. But for all you knew he could've grown in _____ or received a useful reminder.

بِسْمِ اللهِ الرَّحْمٰنِ الرَّحِيْمِ

عَبَسَ وَتَوَلّٰى ۙ ۝١

اَنْ جَآءَهُ الْاَعْمٰى ؕ ۝٢

وَمَا يُدْرِيْكَ لَعَلَّهٗ يَزَّكّٰى ۙ ۝٣

اَوْ يَذَّكَّرُ فَتَنْفَعَهُ الذِّكْرٰى ؕ ۝٤

اَمَّا مَنِ اسْتَغْنٰى ۙ ۝٥

فَاَنْتَ لَهٗ تَصَدّٰى ؕ ۝٦

وَمَا عَلَيْكَ اَلَّا يَزَّكّٰى ؕ ۝٧

وَاَمَّا مَنْ جَآءَكَ يَسْعٰى ۙ ۝٨

وَهُوَ يَخْشٰى ۙ ۝٩

فَاَنْتَ عَنْهُ تَلَهّٰى ۚ ۝١٠

كَلَّاۤ اِنَّهَا تَذْكِرَةٌ ۚ ۝١١

فَمَنْ شَآءَ ذَكَرَهٗ ۘ ۝١٢

فِيْ صُحُفٍ مُّكَرَّمَةٍ ۙ ۝١٣

مَّرْفُوْعَةٍ مُّطَهَّرَةٍ ۢ ۙ ۝١٤

بِاَيْدِيْ سَفَرَةٍ ۙ ۝١٥

كِرَامٍ بَرَرَةٍ ؕ ۝١٦

قُتِلَ الْإِنْسَانُ مَا أَكْفَرَهُ ۝

مِنْ أَيِّ شَيْءٍ خَلَقَهُ ۝

مِنْ نُّطْفَةٍ خَلَقَهُ فَقَدَّرَهُ ۝

ثُمَّ السَّبِيلَ يَسَّرَهُ ۝

ثُمَّ أَمَاتَهُ فَأَقْبَرَهُ ۝

ثُمَّ إِذَا شَاءَ أَنْشَرَهُ ۝

كَلَّا لَمَّا يَقْضِ مَا أَمَرَهُ ۝

فَلْيَنْظُرِ الْإِنْسَانُ إِلَى طَعَامِهِ ۝

أَنَّا صَبَبْنَا الْمَاءَ صَبًّا ۝

ثُمَّ شَقَقْنَا الْاَرْضَ شَقًّا ۝

فَاَنْبَتْنَا فِيْهَا حَبًّا ۝

وَّعِنَبًا وَّقَضْبًا ۝

وَّزَيْتُوْنًا وَّنَخْلًا ۝

وَّحَدَآئِقَ غُلْبًا ۝

وَّفَاكِهَةً وَّاَبًّا ۝

مَّتَاعًا لَّكُمْ وَلِاَنْعَامِكُمْ ۝

فَاِذَا جَآءَتِ الصَّآخَّةُ ۝

42

يَوْمَ يَفِرُّ الْمَرْءُ مِنْ أَخِيهِ ۞

وَأُمِّهِ وَأَبِيهِ ۞

وَصَاحِبَتِهِ وَبَنِيهِ ۞

لِكُلِّ امْرِئٍ مِّنْهُمْ يَوْمَئِذٍ شَأْنٌ يُّغْنِيهِ ۞

وُجُوهٌ يَوْمَئِذٍ مُّسْفِرَةٌ ۞

ضَاحِكَةٌ مُّسْتَبْشِرَةٌ ۞

وَوُجُوهٌ يَوْمَئِذٍ عَلَيْهَا غَبَرَةٌ ۞

تَرْهَقُهَا قَتَرَةٌ ۞

أُولَٰئِكَ هُمُ الْكَفَرَةُ الْفَجَرَةُ ۞

Surah 80 Transliteration

Bismillahir Rahmanir Rahim

1. 'Abasa wa tawwalla

2. An jaa-ahul 'amaa.

3. Wa maa yudreeka la'al lahoo yazzak kaa.

4. Ow yadh dhak karu fa tanfa'ahul dhikraa.

5. Ammaa man istaghnaa.

6. Fa anta lahu tasad daa.

7. Wa maa 'alayka allaa yazzak kaa.

8. Wa ammaa man jaa-aka yas'aa.

9. Wa huwa yakhshaa.

10. Fa anta 'anhu talah haa.

11. Kallaa innahaa tadh kerah.

12. Fa man shaa-a dhakarah.

13. Fee suhufim mukarramah.

14. Marfoo 'atin mutah harah.

15. Be aiydee safarah.

16. Kiraamin bara rah.

17. Qutilal insaanu maa akfarah.

18. Min aiyye shaiy-in khalaqah?

19. Min nutfatin khalaqahu fa qaddarah.

20. Thoommas sabeela yassarah.

21. Thoomma amaatahoo fa aqbarah.

22. Thoomma edhaa sha-a ansharah.

23. Kallaa lammaa yaqde maa amarah.

24. Fal yandhuril insaanu elaa taw 'aamih.

25. Annaa sababnal maa -asabba.

26. Thoomma shaqawqnal -arda shaqqaa.

27. Fa anbatna feehaa habbaa.

28. Wa 'enabaw wa qad baa.

29. Wa zaytoonaw wa nakhla.

30. Wa hadaa-eqa ghulbaa.

31. Wa faakehataw wa abbaa.

32. Mataa 'al lakum wa le an 'aamekum.

33. Fa edhaa jaa-atis sawkh khah.

34. Yowma yafirrul mar-u min akheeh.

35. Wa ummehe wa abeeh.

36. Wa sawhibatihe wa baneeh.

37. Le kul lim re-im minhum yowma -edhin sha-nuey yughneeh.

38. Wujuhoey yowma -edhin musfirah.

39. Daw hekatum mustab shirah.

40. Wa wujuhoey yowma -edhin 'alayhaa gha barah.

41. Tar haquhaa qatarah.

42. Oola-ika hoomul kafaratul fajara.

The Enveloping

81 At Takwīr
Early Meccan Period

🔍 BACKGROUND

The idol-worshippers of Mecca could not explain the source of the Prophet's revelations. So they started to say that a devil lived in him or that he was crazy. This was a silly thing to say when the Prophet was calling people to be good and to control themselves. This chapter gave the Prophet a way to reply to the idol-worshippers. It begins by describing the terrible things that will happen on the last day before Judgment Day.

*In the Name of Allah,
the Compassionate, the Merciful*

When the sun is covered in darkness, * when the stars are cast down, * when the mountains pass away, * when the farm animals heavy with young are abandoned, * when the wild beasts are herded together, * when the seas rise, * when the souls are sorted, * when the baby girl buried alive is asked for what crime she was killed. [1-8]

When the **scrolls** are opened, * when the sky is laid bare, * and when Hell is set ablaze * and the Garden is brought near, * then every soul will know what it has prepared. [9-14]

And so, by the (stars and planets) that go down, * move on directly or hide, * and by the night as it draws to a close * and by the dawn as it slowly exhales, * (by these signs know that) these are the words of an **honored** messenger. [15-19]

He has authority and status before the Lord of the throne, * and he is to be obeyed and trusted. [20-21]

Your companion (Muhammad) is not crazy, nor is he being **tricked**, * for he certainly saw the (angel of revelation) on a clear horizon. * He doesn't delay in talking about the knowledge of the unseen, * nor are these the words of an accursed devil. [22-25]

So which **way** will you go? [26]

This is no less than a reminder to all the worlds, * for anyone who seeks to walk the straight path – * but not as you decide, as Allah decides, the Lord of All the Worlds. [27-29]

Think About It

1. The idol-worshippers of Arabia used to bury baby girls in the sand if they did not want more children. They thought that girls were not as important as the boys. On the Day of Judgment, what will the baby girls be asked, and why do you think the question is asked like that? (See Verse 8)

2. What does this chapter say about the Prophet when the idol-worshippers said he was crazy?

3. Who can benefit from the Qur'an, according to verses 27-29?

Fill in the Words on the lines below.
Look at the **BOLD** words in the main text to see where they go

Words to Use

Honored   Tricked   Scrolls   Way

---

1. Your companion (Muhammad) is not crazy, nor is he being _____ for he certainly saw the (angel of revelation) on a clear horizon

2. When the _____ are opened...

3. So which _____ will you go?.

4. ...(by these signs know that) these are the words of an _____ messenger.

بِسْمِ اللهِ الرَّحْمٰنِ الرَّحِيْمِ

إِذَا الشَّمْسُ كُوِّرَتْ ۝١

وَإِذَا النُّجُوْمُ انْكَدَرَتْ ۝٢

وَإِذَا الْجِبَالُ سُيِّرَتْ ۝٣

وَإِذَا الْعِشَارُ عُطِّلَتْ ۝٤

وَإِذَا الْوُحُوْشُ حُشِرَتْ ۝٥

وَإِذَا الْبِحَارُ سُجِّرَتْ ۝٦

وَإِذَا النُّفُوْسُ زُوِّجَتْ ۝٧

وَإِذَا الْمَوْءُدَةُ سُئِلَتْ ۝٨

بِأَيِّ ذَنۢبٍ قُتِلَتۡ ۝

وَإِذَا الصُّحُفُ نُشِرَتۡ ۝

وَإِذَا السَّمَآءُ كُشِطَتۡ ۝

وَإِذَا الۡجَحِيمُ سُعِّرَتۡ ۝

وَإِذَا الۡجَنَّةُ أُزۡلِفَتۡ ۝

عَلِمَتۡ نَفۡسٌ مَّآ أَحۡضَرَتۡ ۝

فَلَآ أُقۡسِمُ بِالۡخُنَّسِ ۝

الۡجَوَارِ الۡكُنَّسِ ۝

وَالَّيۡلِ إِذَا عَسۡعَسَ ۝

وَالصُّبْحِ إِذَا تَنَفَّسَ ۝ ⁨١٨⁩

إِنَّهُ لَقَوْلُ رَسُولٍ كَرِيمٍ ۝ ⁨١٩⁩

ذِى قُوَّةٍ عِنْدَ ذِى الْعَرْشِ مَكِينٍ ۝ ⁨٢٠⁩

مُّطَاعٍ ثَمَّ أَمِينٍ ۝ ⁨٢١⁩

وَمَا صَاحِبُكُمْ بِمَجْنُونٍ ۝ ⁨٢٢⁩

وَلَقَدْ رَآهُ بِالْأُفُقِ الْمُبِينِ ۝ ⁨٢٣⁩

وَمَا هُوَ عَلَى الْغَيْبِ بِضَنِينٍ ۝ ⁨٢٤⁩

وَمَا هُوَ بِقَوْلِ شَيْطَنٍ رَّجِيمٍ ۝ ⁨٢٥⁩

فَأَيْنَ تَذْهَبُونَ ۝ ⁨٢٦⁩

إِنْ هُوَ إِلَّا ذِكْرٌ لِّلْعَلَمِينَ ۝ ⁨٢٧⁩

لِمَنْ شَاءَ مِنْكُمْ أَنْ يَّسْتَقِيمَ ۝ ⁨٢٨⁩

وَمَا تَشَاءُونَ إِلَّا أَنْ يَّشَاءَ اللهُ رَبُّ الْعَلَمِينَ ۝ ⁨٢٩⁩

Surah 81 Transliteration

Bismillahir Rahmanir Rahim

1. Edhas shamsu kuwwirat.

2. Wa edhan nujumun kadarat.

3. Wa edhal jibaalu sooyyerat.

4. Wa edhal 'ishaaru 'oot tilat.

5. Wa edhal wuhushu hushirat.

6. Wa edhal bihaaru sujjirat.

7. Wa edhan nufusu zuw wejat.

8. Wa edhal mow-oodatu su-elat.

9. Be aiyye dhanbin qutilat.

10. Wa edhas suhufu nushirat.

11. Wa edhas sama-u kushitat.

12. Wa edhal jaheemu su' 'irat.

13. Wa edhal jannatu uz lefat.

14. 'Alimat nafsun maa ah darat.

15. Falaa ooq semu bil khun nas.

16. Al jawaaril kun nas.

17. Wal laiyle edha 'as 'as.

18. Was soob he edha tanaf fas.

53

19. Innahu laqowlu rasoolin kareem.

20. Dhee quwwatin 'inda dheel 'arshi makeen.

21. Mootaw'in thamma ameen.

22. Wa maa sawhibukum be majnoon.

23. Wa laqad ra aa hoo bil oofuqeel mubeen.

24. Wa maa huwa 'alaal ghaiybe be dawneen.

25. Wa maa huwa be qowle shaiytanir rajeem.

26. Fa aiyna tadh haboon?

27. In huwa illaa dhikrul lil 'aalameen.

28. Leman sha-a minkum aiy yastaqeem.

29. Wa maa tashaa-oona illaa aiy yasha-allahu rabbul 'aalameen.

The Dividing

82 Al Infitār
Early Meccan Period

🔍 <u>BACKGROUND</u>

The idol-worshippers did not believe that their good and bad deeds were important. They thought that Allah was far away, and that their idols were like mini-gods who would help them. This chapter introduced to them the idea that all their deeds would be looked at on a final Day of Judgment.

*In the Name of Allah,
the Compassionate, the Merciful*

When the skies are divided * and the stars are dispersed, * when the oceans overflow * and the graves are overturned, * then every soul will know what it has sent ahead and left behind. [1-5]

O People! What has taken you away from your Generous Lord - * the One Who created you (in the womb), balanced you (in proportion), gave you a sense of justice * and made you in whatever form He wished? [6-8]

But no! Certainly not! Even still you deny the judgment (to come)! * (You should know) that guardians (are set to watch) over you. * (They're) the noble recorders * who know everything you do. [9-12]

The good *people* will be in joy, * even as the arrogant *people* will burn in the flames. [13-14]

They're going to enter it on the Day of Judgment, * and they won't be able to avoid it. [15-16]

So how can you appreciate (the importance) of the Day of Judgment, * and how can you understand what the Day of Judgment will be? [17-18]

On that day, no soul will be able to help another one at all. (On that day), all power to command will belong to only Allah. [19]

⛅ Think About It

1. Why do you think there are guardians who watch over us?

2. In what way does Allah try to convince us to believe in Him, in verses 6-8?

3. Why do you think that good people get rewarded and bad people get punished?

4. Write down three good deeds that you think Allah will like for a believer to do.

     A.

     B.

     C.

     D.

5. Which one is the easiest for people to do, and why?

6. Muslims are asked to share Islam with others. Think of a way you might tell a non-Muslim about Islam. What could you say to get them interested to know more?

بِسْمِ اللهِ الرَّحْمٰنِ الرَّحِيمِ

إِذَا السَّمَاءُ انْفَطَرَتْ ۝١

وَإِذَا الْكَوَاكِبُ انْتَثَرَتْ ۝٢

وَإِذَا الْبِحَارُ فُجِّرَتْ ۝٣

وَإِذَا الْقُبُورُ بُعْثِرَتْ ۝٤

عَلِمَتْ نَفْسٌ مَّا قَدَّمَتْ وَ أَخَّرَتْ ۝٥

يَا أَيُّهَا الْإِنْسَانُ مَا غَرَّكَ بِرَبِّكَ الْكَرِيمِ ۝٦

الَّذِي خَلَقَكَ فَسَوَّىٰكَ فَعَدَلَكَ ۝٧

فِي أَيِّ صُورَةٍ مَّا شَاءَ رَكَّبَكَ ۝٨

كَلَّا بَلْ تُكَذِّبُونَ بِالدِّينِ ۝

وَإِنَّ عَلَيْكُمْ لَحَافِظِينَ ۝

كِرَامًا كَاتِبِينَ ۝

يَعْلَمُونَ مَا تَفْعَلُونَ ۝

إِنَّ الْأَبْرَارَ لَفِي نَعِيمٍ ۝

وَإِنَّ الْفُجَّارَ لَفِي جَحِيمٍ ۝

يَصْلَوْنَهَا يَوْمَ الدِّينِ ۝

وَمَا هُمْ عَنْهَا بِغَائِبِينَ ۝

وَمَا أَدْرَاكَ مَا يَوْمُ الدِّينِ ۝

ثُمَّ مَا أَدْرَاكَ مَا يَوْمُ الدِّينِ ۝

يَوْمَ لَا تَمْلِكُ نَفْسٌ لِنَفْسٍ شَيْئًا ۖ وَالْأَمْرُ يَوْمَئِذٍ لِلَّهِ ۝

Surah 82 Transliteration

Bismillahir Rahmanir Rahim

1. Edhas samaa-un fatarat.

2. Wa edhal kawakebun tatharat.

3. Wa edhal behaaru fuj jirat.

4. Wa edhal qubooru bu'thirat.

5. 'Alimat nafsun maa qad damat wa akh kharat.

6. Ya aiy yoohal insaanu maa ghar raka be rabbekal kareem?

7. Alladhee khalaqaka fa saw waka fa 'adalak.

8. Fee aiyyee sooratin maa shaa-a rak kabak.

9. Kallaa bal tukadh dheboona bid deen.

10. Wa inna 'alaykum la haafedheen,

11. Kiraamaan kaatibeen.

12. Ya'lamoona maa taf 'aloon.

13. Innal abraara lafee na'eem.

14. Wa innal fuj jaara lafee jaheem.

15. Yas lownaahaa yowmad deen.

16. Wa maa hoom 'anhaa be ghaw-ibeen.

17. Wa maa ad raaka maa yowmud deen?

18. Thoomma maa ad raaka maa yowmud deen?

19. Yowma laa tamliku nafsul le nafsin shaiy-an wal amru yowma -edhil lillah.

The Shortchanger
83 At-Tatfeef
Early Meccan Period

Q BACKGROUND

The first four verse of this chapter were revealed when the Prophet entered Medina and saw that the merchants were being very tricky with their customers. The rest of the chapter had been revealed earlier while he was still living in Mecca.

In the Name of Allah,
the Compassionate, the Merciful

And now a warning to people who shortchange, * who want every last item *from people* when they're owed something, * but who short-change when they have to pay *someone*. [1-3]

Don't they realize they're going to be resurrected * on a super important day - * the day when all people will stand before the Lord of All the Worlds? [4-6]

But no! The record of the bad people is kept in the Crevice, * and how can you understand what the Crevice is? * It's a written record. [7-9]

So destruction that day to those who denied * and (destruction) to those who called the Day of Judgment a lie, * for only the rebellious and wrongdoers deny (the truth). [10-12]

The Faithless Reject the Truth

When Our (revealed) verses are read to one of them, he says, *"Tales from long ago!"* * No way! Not so! Their hearts are rusted by the burden (of the sins) they've earned. [13-14]

No way! They're going to be hidden from the (forgiveness) of their Lord that day, * and then they'll be forced to enter the raging blaze. * Then they'll be told, *"This is what you were so quick to deny!"* [13-17]

Where Allah Keeps the Grades

On the contrary, the record of the righteous is kept in the Summit, * and how can you understand what the Summit is? [18-19]

It's (also) a written record, * witnessed over by those nearest (to Allah). [20-21]

The righteous will be in joy; * gathered upon thrones, they'll be looking around. [22-23]

You'll recognize the glow of delight upon their faces. * They'll be served the finest wine sealed – * it will be sealed with the flavor of musk.

People who like the best things should think (about this delight) and work hard (to achieve it), * for (it's a drink) mixed with pure pleasure, * drawn from a fountain that only those nearest (to Allah) may drink from. [24-28]

hurried back to their associates to laugh and joke, * and whenever they saw them they would say, *"Truly, these are the ones who got it all wrong!"* [29-32]

The wicked used to laugh at those who believed. * They winked at each other whenever they passed by, * then

However, they were not sent to be in charge of them! * Yet, on this day, it will be the believers who will laugh at the faithless * from on top of high thrones. [33-35]

Won't the faithless get their payback for (the bad things) that they did? [36]

☁ Think About It

1. Why is it wrong to cheat people when they buy from you?

2. Allah keeps the record of deeds for all people. The bad people have their records in one place, and the good people have their records in another place. Look up the defintions of Crevace and Summit. Based on what you learn from the dictionary, what is the symbolism of each place and the kinds of records kept there?

3. Wine and other alcoholic drinks are forbidden in this world for a believer, but in Jennah (Paradise) they are not. Why do you think that is?

4. Wine is haram, or forbidden in this life, but in Jennah (Heaven) there will be pure wine that is halal. How is that wine described in this chapter?

5. The Prophet promised that in Jennah we can have whatever our hearts desire. If you make it to Jennah, what is one thing you would love to have, and why?

6. It is hard to a be faithful believer in Allah in a world surrounded by temptations. How do verses 29-36 try to give us strength in this world?

بِسْمِ اللّٰهِ الرَّحْمٰنِ الرَّحِيْمِ

وَيْلٌ لِّلْمُطَفِّفِيْنَ ۙ ١

الَّذِيْنَ اِذَا اكْتَالُوْا عَلَى النَّاسِ يَسْتَوْفُوْنَ ۖ ٢

وَ اِذَا كَالُوْهُمْ اَوْ وَّزَنُوْهُمْ يُخْسِرُوْنَ ؕ ٣

اَلَا يَظُنُّ اُولٰٓئِكَ اَنَّهُمْ مَّبْعُوْثُوْنَ ۙ ٤

لِيَوْمٍ عَظِيْمٍ ۙ ٥

يَّوْمَ يَقُوْمُ النَّاسُ لِرَبِّ الْعٰلَمِيْنَ ؕ ٦

كَلَّا اِنَّ كِتٰبَ الْفُجَّارِ لَفِيْ سِجِّيْنٍ ؕ ٧

وَ مَا اَدْرٰىكَ مَا سِجِّيْنٌ ؕ ٨

كِتٰبٌ مَّرْقُوْمٌ ؕ ٩

وَيْلٌ يَّوْمَئِذٍ لِّلْمُكَذِّبِيْنَ ۙ ١٠

الَّذِيْنَ يُكَذِّبُوْنَ بِيَوْمِ الدِّيْنِ ؕ ١١

وَ مَا يُكَذِّبُ بِهٖٓ اِلَّا كُلُّ مُعْتَدٍ اَثِيْمٍ ۙ ١٢

اِذَا تُتْلٰى عَلَيْهِ اٰيٰتُنَا قَالَ اَسَاطِيْرُ الْاَوَّلِيْنَ ؕ ١٣

كَلَّا بَلْ رَانَ عَلَىٰ قُلُوبِهِم مَّا كَانُوا يَكْسِبُونَ ﴿١٤﴾

كَلَّا إِنَّهُمْ عَن رَّبِّهِمْ يَوْمَئِذٍ لَّمَحْجُوبُونَ ﴿١٥﴾

ثُمَّ إِنَّهُمْ لَصَالُوا الْجَحِيمِ ﴿١٦﴾

ثُمَّ يُقَالُ هَٰذَا الَّذِي كُنتُم بِهِ تُكَذِّبُونَ ﴿١٧﴾

كَلَّا إِنَّ كِتَابَ الْأَبْرَارِ لَفِي عِلِّيِّينَ ﴿١٨﴾

وَمَا أَدْرَاكَ مَا عِلِّيُّونَ ﴿١٩﴾

كِتَابٌ مَّرْقُومٌ ﴿٢٠﴾

يَشْهَدُهُ الْمُقَرَّبُونَ ﴿٢١﴾

إِنَّ الْأَبْرَارَ لَفِي نَعِيمٍ ﴿٢٢﴾

عَلَى الْأَرَائِكِ يَنظُرُونَ ﴿٢٣﴾

تَعْرِفُ فِي وُجُوهِهِمْ نَضْرَةَ النَّعِيمِ ﴿٢٤﴾

يُسْقَوْنَ مِن رَّحِيقٍ مَّخْتُومٍ ﴿٢٥﴾

67

خِتٰمُهٗ مِسْكٌ ۚ وَفِیْ ذٰلِكَ فَلْیَتَنَافَسِ الْمُتَنَافِسُوْنَ ۙ ۲۶

وَمِزَاجُهٗ مِنْ تَسْنِیْمٍ ۙ ۲۷

عَیْنًا یَّشْرَبُ بِهَا الْمُقَرَّبُوْنَ ؕ ۲۸

اِنَّ الَّذِیْنَ اَجْرَمُوْا کَانُوْا مِنَ الَّذِیْنَ اٰمَنُوْا یَضْحَکُوْنَ ۫ ۲۹

وَاِذَا مَرُّوْا بِهِمْ یَتَغَامَزُوْنَ ۫ ۳۰

وَاِذَا انْقَلَبُوْۤا اِلٰۤی اَهْلِهِمُ انْقَلَبُوْا فَکِهِیْنَ ۫ ۳۱

وَاِذَا رَاَوْهُمْ قَالُوْۤا اِنَّ هٰۤؤُلَآءِ لَضَآلُّوْنَ ۙ ۳۲

وَمَاۤ اُرْسِلُوْا عَلَیْهِمْ حٰفِظِیْنَ ؕ ۳۳

فَالْیَوْمَ الَّذِیْنَ اٰمَنُوْا مِنَ الْکُفَّارِ یَضْحَکُوْنَ ۙ ۳۴

عَلَی الْاَرَآئِكِ یَنْظُرُوْنَ ؕ ۳۵

هَلْ ثُوِّبَ الْکُفَّارُ مَا کَانُوْا یَفْعَلُوْنَ ۳۶

Surah 83 Transliteration

1. Waiy lul lil mutaf fefeen.

2. Alladheena edhak taaloo 'alaan naase yastowfoon.

3. Wa edha kaaluhum ow wazanuhoom yookh seroon.

4. Alaa yadhunnu oolaa-eka annahoom mab 'oothoon.

5. Le yowmin 'owdheem.

6. Yowma yaqoomun naasu lerabbil 'aalameen.

7. Kallaa inna kitaabal fuj jaari lafee sij jeen.

8. Wa maa ad raaka maa sij jeen?

9. Kitaabun marqoom.

10. Waiylun yowma -edhin lil mukadh dhebeen.

11. Alladheena yukadh dheboona be yowmid deen.

12. Wa maa yukadh dhebu behe illaa kulloo mu'tadin atheem.

13. Edha tootlaa 'alayhe ayaatuna qawla asaatirul owwaleen.

14. Kallaa bal raana 'alaa quloobehim maa kaanu yak seboon.

15. Kallaa innahum 'ar rabbihim yowma -edhil lamah joo boon.

16. Thoomma innahum lasawlul jaheem.

17. Thoomma yuqawlu haadhal ladhee kuntum behe tukadh dheboon.

18. Kalla inna kitaabal abraari lafee 'illeyeen.

19. Wa maa ad raaka maa 'illeyoon?

20. Kitaabun marqoom.

21. Yash haduhul muqar raboon.

22. Innal abraara lafee na'eem.

23. 'Alaal araa-eke yan dhuroon.

24. Ta'rifoo fee wujoohehim nadratan na'eem.

25. Yusqowna min raheeqin makh toom.

26. Khitamuhu miskun wa fee dhaalika fal yatana faseel muta naafisoon.

27. Wa mizaajuhu min tasneem.

28. 'Aiy naiy yashraboo behaal muqar raboon.

29. Innal lladheena ajramoo kaanoo minal ladheena amanoo yad hakoon.

30. Wa edha mar roo behim yata ghaw mazoon.

31. Wa edhan qalaboo elaa ah lehimun qalaboo fakeheen.

32. Wa edha ra owhoom qawloo inna ha-oola-ee ladaawlloon.

33. Wa maa urseloo 'alayhim hafidheen.

34. Fal yowmal ladheena aamanoo minal kuffaare yad hakoon.

35. 'Alal araa-eki yandhuroon.

36. Hal thoowebal kuffaaru maa kanoo yaf'aloon?

The Tearing

84 Al Inshiqāq
Early Meccan Period

🔍 BACKGROUND

This chapter was revealed to the Prophet before he started preaching in public. It had a simple and direct message that said people must be careful of their deeds. Allah is watching over all things and He will not forget the good and the bad that we do.

In the Name of Allah,
the Compassionate, the Merciful

When the sky is torn away * by the will of its Lord, which it must obey, * when the earth is leveled * and throws out all it contains * by the will of its Lord, which it must obey, * then all you human beings, who have been struggling on the journey towards your Lord, will finally meet Him! [1-6]

Then, the one who receives their record in their right hand * will soon have an easy review. * They will return to their people **celebrating**. [7-9]

But the one who receives their record from behind their back * will soon wish to be destroyed * as they're driven into the raging blaze. [10-12]

Truly, they spent their life celebrating with their people, * never thinking they'd be (brought before their Creator) in the end. * But no! Their Lord was always **watching** him. [13-15]

And so by the fleeting afterglow of sunset, * by the night and what it conceals * and by the moon as it grows full, * (know by these same tokens) that you're certainly progressing in stages. [16-19]

> **Q BACKGROUND**
>
> After reading verses 20-21 below, it is customary for the one who has faith in Allah to prostrate him or herself on the floor and praise Allah.
> (Ma'ariful Qur'an)

So what's the matter with them that they don't believe, * and why don't they bow themselves in wonder upon hearing the Qur'an read to them? [20-21]

But no! The faithless just **deny** it like that! * Allah knows their innermost thoughts, * so give them the news of a painful doom. [22-24]

However, for those who believe and do what's good and right, there's a **reward** that will never end. [25]

☁️ Think About It

1. How do you think people will feel when they arrive for the Day of Judgment?

2. Why do righteous and good people get an 'easy review' on Judhment Day?

3. Verses 10-15 mention the quality of a person who does not care about the meaning of life and their fate in the next life. What ar some ways that people can live life ignoring the truth and 'celebrating' with their people? Give two examples.

Fill in the Words on the lines below.
Look at the **BOLD** words in the main text to see where they go

Words to Use

Deny   Celebrating   Reward   Watching

---

1. His Lord was always _____ him.

2. However, for those who believe and do what's good and right, there's a _____ that will never end.

3. The faithless just _____ it like that!

4. He will return to his people _____.

بِسْمِ اللهِ الرَّحْمٰنِ الرَّحِيْمِ

اِذَا السَّمَآءُ انْشَقَّتْ ۝١

وَاَذِنَتْ لِرَبِّهَا وَحُقَّتْ ۝٢

وَاِذَا الْاَرْضُ مُدَّتْ ۝٣

وَاَلْقَتْ مَا فِيْهَا وَتَخَلَّتْ ۝٤

وَاَذِنَتْ لِرَبِّهَا وَحُقَّتْ ۝٥

يٰٓاَيُّهَا الْاِنْسَانُ اِنَّكَ كَادِحٌ
اِلٰى رَبِّكَ كَدْحًا فَمُلٰقِيْهِ ۝٦

فَاَمَّا مَنْ اُوْتِيَ كِتٰبَهٗ بِيَمِيْنِهٖ ۝٧

فَسَوْفَ يُحَاسَبُ حِسَابًا يَّسِيْرًا ۝٨

وَّيَنْقَلِبُ اِلٰٓى اَهْلِهٖ مَسْرُوْرًا ۝٩

وَاَمَّا مَنْ اُوْتِيَ كِتٰبَهٗ وَرَآءَ ظَهْرِهٖ ۝١٠

فَسَوْفَ يَدْعُوْا ثُبُوْرًا ۝١١

وَّيَصْلٰى سَعِيْرًا ۝١٢

75

اِنَّهُ كَانَ فِىٓ اَهْلِهٖ مَسْرُوْرًا ۝

اِنَّهُ ظَنَّ اَنْ لَّنْ يَّحُوْرَ ۝

بَلٰىٓ ۚ اِنَّ رَبَّهُ كَانَ بِهٖ بَصِيْرًا ۝

فَلَآ اُقْسِمُ بِالشَّفَقِ ۝

وَالَّيْلِ وَمَا وَسَقَ ۝

وَالْقَمَرِ اِذَا اتَّسَقَ ۝

لَتَرْكَبُنَّ طَبَقًا عَنْ طَبَقٍ ۝

فَمَا لَهُمْ لَا يُؤْمِنُوْنَ ۝

وَاِذَا قُرِئَ عَلَيْهِمُ الْقُرْاٰنُ لَا يَسْجُدُوْنَ ۩ ۝

بَلِ الَّذِيْنَ كَفَرُوْا يُكَذِّبُوْنَ ۝

وَاللّٰهُ اَعْلَمُ بِمَا يُوْعُوْنَ ۝

فَبَشِّرْهُمْ بِعَذَابٍ اَلِيْمِ ۝

اِلَّا الَّذِيْنَ اٰمَنُوْا وَعَمِلُوا الصّٰلِحٰتِ

لَهُمْ اَجْرٌ غَيْرُ مَمْنُوْنٍ ۝

Bismillahir Rahmanir Rahim

1. Edhas samaa-un shaq qat.

2. Wa adhinat lerabbehaa wa huq qat.

3. Wa edhal -ardu mood dat.

4. Wa alqat maa feehaa wa takhallat.

5. Wa -adhinat lee rabbiha wa huq qat.

6. Ya aiy yuhal insaanu innaka kaadihun elaa rabbika kad haan fa mulaaqeeh.

7. Fa ammaa man ooteya kitaabahu be yameeneh.

8. Fa sowfa yuhaasabu hesaabaiy yaseera.

9. Wa yanqalibu elaa ah lehe masroora.

10. Wa amma man ootiya kitaabahu wara-a dhahreh.

11. Fa sowfa yad'oo thuboora.

12. Wa yaslaa sa'eera.

13. Innahoo kaana fee ah lehe masroora.

14. Innahoo dhanna an laiy yahoor.

15. Balaa inna rabbahu kaana behe baseera.

16. Fa laa ooq semu bish shafaq.

17. Wal laiyle wa maa wasaq.

18. Wal qamare edhat tasaq.

19. La tarkabunna tabaqaan 'an tabaq.

20. Fa maa lahoom laa yu'menoon?

21. Wa edha qoori-a 'alayhimul qur-aanu laa yasjudoon? *

* *(Face Mecca and bow once after reading the above line.)*

22. Balil ladheena kafaroo yukadh dheboon.

23. Wallaahu 'alamu bemaa yoo'oon.

24. Fa bash shirhum be 'adhaabin 'aleem.

25. Illal ladheena aamanoo wa 'amiloos sawlihaati lahoom ajrun ghairu mam noon.

The Constellations

85 Al Burooj
Early Meccan Period

🔍 BACKGROUND

This chapter talks about the story of some people in the land of Yemen, which was located at the lower end of Arabia. There was a Jewish king named Dhu Nuwas who had an old wizard.

The wizard asked for a student, so the king arranged for a young boy to visit him every day to learn magic. On the road to the wizard's house, the boy met an old Christian man who also started to teach him about Prophet Jesus.

So the boy had two teachers – one in the morning and one in the evening, and both teachers taught him opposite things. The old man asked the boy to keep his teachings and home a secret.

One day, the boy decided that he liked the teachings of the Christian man better, and he gave up magic. He started teaching the people to be good and kind like Prophet Jesus was. The king was angry when he learned about this, and he tried to kill the boy, but Allah kept saving him.

The boy tricked the king into telling a crowd that his teachings were the best to follow, and the boy gave his life to make this plan work. Then lots of people wanted to follow the teachings of the boy.

The king got even *more* angry and ordered his soldiers to throw the believers into fire pits. This chapter mentions that time in history and tells how bad people will be punished for hurting innocent people.

In the Name of Allah,
the Compassionate, the Merciful

By the sky filled with constellations, * by the Promised Day (of Judgment) * and by the witness (which is Friday) and all that it witnesses. [1-3]

(By these same tokens know that) the pit-diggers will be ruined, * (for they tried to destroy the believers) with a well-fed fire. * They gathered around it * and saw full well what they were doing to the believers. [4-7]

They were hurting them for no other reason than that they had faith in Allah, the Most High and Praised One, * the One Whose kingdom extends over the heavens and the earth, and Allah is a witness to all things. [8-9]

For sure, those who hurt the believing men and the believing women like that, and who don't say sorry (for doing those bad things), they will be punished with the fires of Hell, and in that way they will be punished with (an even greater) fire! [10]

Those who believe and do what's good and right will have gardens beneath which rivers flow – *and that's the greatest success of all!* [11]

81

Truly, your Lord has a firm grip. * He starts (the creation) and gives (life back to the dead). [12-13]

(Allah) is the Forgiving and the Loving - * the Lord of the throne of glory * and Doer of all He wants to do! [14-16]

Have you ever heard of the stories of the big crowds * of Pharaoh and of the (people of) Thamud? [17-18]

But no! The faithless still keep going in their rejection. * Yet, Allah is right behind them! [19-20]

Even though (they keep rejecting it), this is a Noble Qur'an * (that's forever kept) on a protected tablet. [21-22]

 **Think About It**

1. Look at this map of Arabia to the right.

The Middle East

- Circle the land of Yemen

- Draw a line under the name of Abyssinia

- Draw a square around the name "Arabia."

- What is the name of the Empire to the NORTH of Arabia?

- Which foreign country in those days do you think would have more influence in Arabia and why?

2. Why did the evil pit-diggers harm the believers?

3. Where does Allah keep the original Qur'an *preserved* forever? (Hint: on a t_____.)

4. In our modern world, there are times when the believers are also harmed because they say they are Muslims. Ask someone in your family, a teacher or use the internet to look up the name of a tragedy Muslims suffered in recent times. Give the name here, and describe in one paragraph why it happened (or is happening).

بِسْمِ اللَّهِ الرَّحْمَٰنِ الرَّحِيمِ

وَالسَّمَاءِ ذَاتِ الْبُرُوجِ ۝١

وَالْيَوْمِ الْمَوْعُودِ ۝٢

وَشَاهِدٍ وَّمَشْهُودٍ ۝٣

قُتِلَ أَصْحَابُ الْأُخْدُودِ ۝٤

النَّارِ ذَاتِ الْوَقُودِ ۝٥

إِذْ هُمْ عَلَيْهَا قُعُودٌ ۝٦

وَّهُمْ عَلَىٰ مَا يَفْعَلُونَ بِالْمُؤْمِنِينَ شُهُودٌ ۝٧

وَمَا نَقَمُوا مِنْهُمْ إِلَّا أَنْ يُّؤْمِنُوا بِاللَّهِ الْعَزِيزِ الْحَمِيدِ ۝٨

الَّذِي لَهُ مُلْكُ السَّمَاوَاتِ وَالْأَرْضِ ۖ

وَاللَّهُ عَلَىٰ كُلِّ شَيْءٍ شَهِيدٌ ۝٩

إِنَّ الَّذِينَ فَتَنُوا الْمُؤْمِنِينَ وَالْمُؤْمِنَاتِ ثُمَّ لَمْ يَتُوبُوا

فَلَهُمْ عَذَابُ جَهَنَّمَ وَلَهُمْ عَذَابُ الْحَرِيقِ ۝١٠

إِنَّ الَّذِيْنَ اٰمَنُوْا وَعَمِلُوا الصّٰلِحٰتِ لَهُمْ جَنّٰتٌ تَجْرِىْ مِنْ تَحْتِهَا الْاَنْهٰرُ ؕ ذٰلِكَ الْفَوْزُ الْكَبِيْرُ ۝

إِنَّ بَطْشَ رَبِّكَ لَشَدِيْدٌ ؕ ۝

إِنَّهٗ هُوَ يُبْدِئُ وَيُعِيْدُ ۚ ۝

وَهُوَ الْغَفُوْرُ الْوَدُوْدُ ۙ ۝

ذُو الْعَرْشِ الْمَجِيْدُ ۙ ۝

فَعَّالٌ لِّمَا يُرِيْدُ ؕ ۝

هَلْ اَتٰىكَ حَدِيْثُ الْجُنُوْدِ ۙ ۝

فِرْعَوْنَ وَثَمُوْدَ ؕ ۝

بَلِ الَّذِيْنَ كَفَرُوْا فِيْ تَكْذِيْبٍ ۙ ۝

وَّاللّٰهُ مِنْ وَّرَآئِهِمْ مُّحِيْطٌ ۚ ۝

بَلْ هُوَ قُرْاٰنٌ مَّجِيْدٌ ۙ ۝

فِيْ لَوْحٍ مَّحْفُوْظٍ ۟ ۝

85

Surah 85 Transliteration

Bismillahir Rahmanir Rahim

1. Wa samaa-i dhaatil burooj.

2. Wal yowmil mow'ood.

3. Wa shaahidin wa mash hood.

4. Qutila as haabul ookh dood.

5. An naari dhaatil waqood.

6. Idh hoom 'alayhaa qo'ood.

7. Wa hoom 'alaa maa yaf'aloona bil mu-mineena shuhood.

8. Wa maa naqamoo min hoom illaa aiy yu-minu bil lahil 'azeezil hameed.

9. Alladhee lahoo mulkus samaawaati wal -ard. Wallahu 'alaa kul lee shaiy-in shaheed.

10. Innal ladheena fatanool mu-mineena wal mu-minaati thoomma lam yatuboo falahoom 'adhaabu jahannama wa lahoom 'adhaabul hareeq.

11. Innal ladheena aamanoo wa 'amiloos sawlihaati lahum jannatun tajre min tah tihaal anhaar. Dhaalikal fowzul kabeer.

12. Inna batu sha rabbika la shadeed.

13. Innahu huwa yubde-oo wa yu'eed.

14. Wa huwal ghafirul wadood.

15. Dhul 'arshil Majeed.

16. Fa 'aaloon lemaa yooreed.

17. Hal ataaka hadeethul junood?

18. Fir 'aowna wa thamood?

19. Balil ladheena kafaroo fee tak dheeb.

20. Wallahu min waraa-i-him mooheet.

21. Bal huwa Qur-aanun Majeed,

22. Fee louw him mah foothz.

The Night Star

86 At-Tāriq
Early Meccan Period

🔍 BACKGROUND

This chapter was revealed at a time when the Prophet was sharing Islam only with close relatives. He was sitting and having dinner with his uncle Abu Talib ine night, when a shooting star flew across the sky above them.

Abu Talib became scared, because the Arabs used to believe that a shooting star might have a bad effect on someone's life. "What does it mean?" Abu Talib asked.

The Prophet said that it was only a sign from Allah's creation, and nothing more. Abu Talib asked the Prophet what he meant by that, and then this chapter came to the Prophet's mind and he recited it.

In the Name of Allah,
the Compassionate, the Merciful

By the sky and the visitor by night,
* and how can you understand what
the visitor by night is? [1-2]

It's the bright star (that shines
through the midnight sky). * (By this
same token, know that) there is no
soul without a guardian set over it. [3-4]

Now let (every) human being consider what he was created from, * for he was created from a drop of fluid * that comes from between the spine and the rib cage. [5-7]

Truly, (the One Who created people in this way once before) can surely bring them back again * on the day when all secrets will be exposed, * and when they'll have no power or anyone to help them. [8-10]

And so, by the sky as it returns (after completing its cycle) * and by the opening of the earth (by plants and springs), * truly, this speech sorts (the truth from falsehood), * and it's not some kind of game. [11-14]

(Even though the faithless) continue to make their plans, * I'm making a plan, also. * So give the faithless some time, and leave them alone (for a while). [15-17]

☁ Think About It

1. How does Allah emphasize to us that we are all being watched, according to verses 1-4?

2. When a person knows that a higher power is watching, what effect does this have on their behavior and how they interact with other people?

3. We only live for a short time, then the Qur'an says we all return to Allah some day for a review of our life's report card. What argument does this surah make to try and convinve us of that fact?

4. In the box below, draw a picture that demonstrates one part of the message of this surah. Give it a title, and write one sentence that describes what is happening.

بِسْمِ اللهِ الرَّحْمٰنِ الرَّحِيْمِ

وَالسَّمَاءِ وَالطَّارِقِ ۝١

وَمَا أَدْرَاكَ مَا الطَّارِقُ ۝٢

النَّجْمُ الثَّاقِبُ ۝٣

اِنْ كُلُّ نَفْسٍ لَّمَّا عَلَيْهَا حَافِظٌ ۝٤

فَلْيَنْظُرِ الْإِنْسَانُ مِمَّ خُلِقَ ۝٥

خُلِقَ مِنْ مَّاءٍ دَافِقٍ ۝٦

يَخْرُجُ مِنْ بَيْنِ الصُّلْبِ وَالتَّرَائِبِ ۝٧

اِنَّهُ عَلَى رَجْعِهِ لَقَادِرٌ ۝٨

يَوْمَ تُبْلَى السَّرَائِرُ ۝٩

فَمَا لَهُ مِنْ قُوَّةٍ وَّلَا نَاصِرٍ ۝١٠

وَالسَّمَآءِ ذَاتِ الرَّجْعِ ۞

وَالْاَرْضِ ذَاتِ الصَّدْعِ ۞

اِنَّهُ لَقَوْلٌ فَصْلٌ ۞

وَّمَا هُوَ بِالْهَزْلِ ۞

اِنَّهُمْ يَكِيْدُوْنَ كَيْدًا ۞

وَّاَكِيْدُ كَيْدًا ۞

فَمَهِّلِ الْكٰفِرِيْنَ اَمْهِلْهُمْ رُوَيْدًا ۞

Surah 86 Transliteration

Bismillahir Rahmanir Rahim

1. Wa samaa-i wat taariq.

2. Wa maa ad raaka mat taariq?

3. An najimuth thaaqib.

4. In kul loo nafsil lammaa 'alayhaa haafidh.

5. Fal yandhuril insaanu mimma khuliq?

6. Khuliqa min maa-in daafiq.

7. Yakhruju min baynis sulbi wa taraa-ib.

8. Innahu 'alaa raj 'ehe la qawdir.

9. Yowma tublas saraa-ir.

10. Fa maa lahu min quwwatin wa laa naasir.

11. Was samaa-i dhaatir raj'i.

12. Wal -ardi dhaatis sad'i.

13. Innahu la qowlun fasl.

14. Wa maa huwa bil hazl.

15. Innahoom yakeedoona kaiyda.

16. Wa akeedu kaiyda.

17. Fa mah helil kaafireena amhil hoom ruwaiyda.

The Most High

87 Al A'lā
Early Meccan Period

🔍 BACKGROUND

This is one of the earliest chapter of the Qur'an. At that time, the Prophet was still not used to all the messages he was getting from Angel Jibra'il. He was afraid that he might forget some of the verses or mix them together. This chapter tells him not to worry, because Allah will help him keep everything memorized.

In the Name of Allah,
the Compassionate, the Merciful

Glorify the name of your Lord, the Most High, * the One Who creates and completes (all things), * determines (how long they will exist) and Who directs (them to their end). [1-3]

He's the One Who brings out the lush (green) pastures, * (and He's the One Who) reduces them to dry stalks. [4-5]

We will teach you to recite (this message), so you won't forget anything, * except as Allah wants, for He knows what's out in the open as well as what's hidden away. [6-7]

We'll soon make your path (towards peace of mind) an easy one. * So remind (people), for it may be to their benefit. [8-9]

Whoever is afraid (of making his Lord angry) will take this reminder, * while the bad people will ignore it. * That kind of person is the one who will enter the blazing fire, * and there is no living or dying in there! [10-13]

And so it is that the one who tries to improve himself shall prosper. * He remembers the name of his Lord and prays. [14-15]

But no! It seems that (most of) you still prefer the life of this world, * even though the next life is better and more lasting. [16-17]

Yet, (these truths were revealed) in ancient scrolls before - * in the scrolls of Ibrahim and of Musa. [18-19]

🗨 Think About It

1. According to verses 1-3, how can we describe the power of Allah?

2. What are two ways in which people can respond when they hear about Allah's message?

3. The name for the scrolls of Ibrahim (Abraham) is Suhuf. The Suhuf (Sheets or Leaves) is one of the oldest holy books, though it has been lost long ago. What is the name of one other holy book, besides the Suhuf and the Qur'an? (Hint: look at the picture on page 95 or use your own knowledge.)

4. Based on the picture on page 95, there is another major holy book from Allah, but the name is missing. Find out the name of the missing holy book and write it below.

5. Verse 14 mentions people improving themselves. What is the most important way a person can improve themselves, in your opinion, and how can a person get started on that path?

بِسْمِ اللهِ الرَّحْمٰنِ الرَّحِيْمِ

سَبِّحِ اسْمَ رَبِّكَ الْاَعْلَى ۟١

الَّذِیْ خَلَقَ فَسَوّٰی ۟٢

وَالَّذِیْ قَدَّرَ فَهَدٰی ۟٣

وَالَّذِیْ اَخْرَجَ الْمَرْعٰی ۟٤

فَجَعَلَهٗ غُثَآءً اَحْوٰی ۟٥

سَنُقْرِئُكَ فَلَا تَنْسٰی ۟٦

اِلَّا مَا شَآءَ اللهُ ؕ اِنَّهٗ یَعْلَمُ الْجَهْرَ وَمَا یَخْفٰی ۟٧

وَنُیَسِّرُكَ لِلْیُسْرٰی ۟٨

فَذَكِّرْ اِنْ نَّفَعَتِ الذِّكْرٰی ۟٩

سَیَذَّكَّرُ مَنْ یَّخْشٰی ۟١٠

وَیَتَجَنَّبُهَا الْاَشْقَی ۟١١

الَّذِیْ یَصْلَی النَّارَ الْكُبْرٰی ۟١٢

ثُمَّ لَا یَمُوْتُ فِیْهَا وَلَا یَحْیٰی ۟١٣

97

قَدْ اَفْلَحَ مَنْ تَزَكّٰى ۙ ۝

وَذَكَرَ اسْمَ رَبِّهٖ فَصَلّٰى ؕ ۝

بَلْ تُؤْثِرُوْنَ الْحَيٰوةَ الدُّنْيَا ۖ ۝

وَالْاٰخِرَةُ خَيْرٌ وَّاَبْقٰى ؕ ۝

اِنَّ هٰذَا لَفِى الصُّحُفِ الْاُوْلٰى ۙ ۝

صُحُفِ اِبْرٰهِيْمَ وَمُوْسٰى ۝

Surah 87 Transliteration

Bismillahir Rahmanir Rahim

1. Sabbi hisma rabbikal 'alaa.

2. Alladhee khalaqa fa sawwaa.

3. Wal ladhee qad dara fa hadaa.

4. Wal ladhee akhrajal mar'aa.

5. Fa ja'alahu ghoothaa-an ahwaa.

6. Sa nuqri-uka fa laa tansaa.

7. illaa maa shaa-allahu, in nahu ya'lamul jahra wa maa yakhfaa.

8. Wa nuyas siruka lil yusraa.

9. Fa dhak kir in nafa'atidh dhikraa.

10. Sa yadh dhak karu maiy yakh shaa.

11. Wa yata janna buhaal ashqaw.

12. Alladhee yaslan naaral kubraa.

13. Thoomma laa yamootu feehaa wa laa yahiyaa.

14. Qad aflaha man tazak kaa.

15. Wa dhaka rasma rabbihe fa sallaa.

16. Bal tu-thiroonal hayaatad doonyaa.

17. Wal aakhiratu khaiyrun wa abqaw.

18. Inna hadha lafis suhoofil oolaa.

19. Suhoofi Ebrahema wa Musaa.

The Overwhelming
88 Al Ghawshīyah
Early Meccan Period

In the Name of Allah,
the Compassionate, the Merciful

Have you heard about the overwhelming (event)? * It's the day when some faces will be downcast, * looking worn out and tired * as they're pushed into a raging fire. [1-4]

They'll satisfy their thirst from a boiling spring, * and have no other food than nasty thorn, * which gives no good benefit nor does it taste good. [5-7]

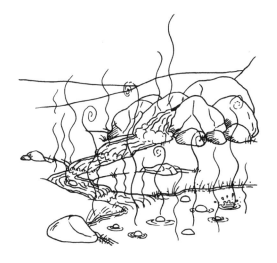

(Other) faces that day will be joyful * and happy with their results. * (They'll be) within high gardens, * hearing no foolish words. [8-11]

A bubbling spring will flow within * and high thrones of honor will be there, too, * with cups placed * and cushions arranged * on rich carpets spread out. [12-16]

Don't (the people who doubt) ever look at the water-filled clouds and wonder about how they were made * or at the sky and how it's been raised up so high * or at the mountains and how they've been set so strong * or at the earth and how it's been spread out so wide? [17-20]

So remind them, (Muhammad,) for you're truly one to remind, * even though you're not in charge (of their hearts). [21-22]

If anyone rejects (the truth) and turns away, * Allah will punish him with a really big punishment. * For sure, they will come back to Us, * and then We will review (all the records). [23-26]

Think About It

1. When the Qur'an describes Jennah and jahennum (Hell) it often gives clear descriptions. How can those clear descriptions influence people to be good?

2. What will the place look like for the good people in Jennah? What kinds of things does this chapter mention?

3. What signs from nature does this chapter ask people to think about?

4. Choose one of the signs from nature mentioned in verses 17-20 and draw a picture of it below in the box.

بِسْمِ اللّٰهِ الرَّحْمٰنِ الرَّحِيْمِ

هَلْ اَتٰىكَ حَدِيْثُ الْغَاشِيَةِ ۚ ۝١

وُجُوهٌ يَّوْمَئِذٍ خَاشِعَةٌ ۙ ۝٢

عَامِلَةٌ نَّاصِبَةٌ ۙ ۝٣

تَصْلٰى نَارًا حَامِيَةً ۙ ۝٤

تُسْقٰى مِنْ عَيْنٍ اٰنِيَةٍ ۚ ۝٥

لَيْسَ لَهُمْ طَعَامٌ اِلَّا مِنْ ضَرِيْعٍ ۙ ۝٦

لَّا يُسْمِنُ وَلَا يُغْنِيْ مِنْ جُوْعٍ ۚ ۝٧

وُجُوهٌ يَّوْمَئِذٍ نَّاعِمَةٌ ۙ ۝٨

لِّسَعْيِهَا رَاضِيَةٌ ۙ ۝٩

فِيْ جَنَّةٍ عَالِيَةٍ ۙ ۝١٠

لَّا تَسْمَعُ فِيْهَا لَاغِيَةً ۗ ۝١١

فِيْهَا عَيْنٌ جَارِيَةٌ ۘ ۝١٢

فِيْهَا سُرُرٌ مَّرْفُوْعَةٌ ۙ ۝١٣

وَّاَكْوَابٌ مَّوْضُوْعَةٌ ۙ ۝١٤

وَّنَمَارِقُ مَصْفُوْفَةٌ ۙ ۝١٥

وَّزَرَابِيُّ مَبْثُوْثَةٌ ۗ ۝١٦

أَفَلَا يَنْظُرُونَ إِلَى الْإِبِلِ كَيْفَ خُلِقَتْ ۩ ﴿١٧﴾

وَإِلَى السَّمَاءِ كَيْفَ رُفِعَتْ ۩ ﴿١٨﴾

وَإِلَى الْجِبَالِ كَيْفَ نُصِبَتْ ۩ ﴿١٩﴾

وَإِلَى الْأَرْضِ كَيْفَ سُطِحَتْ ۩ ﴿٢٠﴾

فَذَكِّرْ ۙ إِنَّمَا أَنْتَ مُذَكِّرٌ ۗ ﴿٢١﴾

لَسْتَ عَلَيْهِمْ بِمُصَيْطِرٍ ﴿٢٢﴾

إِلَّا مَنْ تَوَلَّى وَكَفَرَ ﴿٢٣﴾

فَيُعَذِّبُهُ اللَّهُ الْعَذَابَ الْأَكْبَرَ ۗ ﴿٢٤﴾

إِنَّ إِلَيْنَا إِيَابَهُمْ ﴿٢٥﴾

ثُمَّ إِنَّ عَلَيْنَا حِسَابَهُمْ ﴿٢٦﴾

Surah 88 Transliteration

Bismillahir Rahmanir Rahim

1. Hal ataaka hadeethul ghawshiyah?

2. Wujuhoey yowma -edhin khawshi'ah.

3. 'Aamilatun naasibah.

4. Taslaa naaran haamiyah.

5. Tusqaw min 'aynin aaniyah.

6. Laysa lahoom ta'aamun illaa min da ree'.

7. Laa yusminu wa laa yughnee min joo'.

8. Wujuhoey yowma -edhin naa'imah.

9. Lisa' yehaa raadiyah.

10. Fee jannatin 'aaliyah.

11. Laa tasma'u feehaa laaghiyah.

12. Feehaa 'aynun jaariyah.

13. Feehaa su rurun marfu'ah.

14. Wa akwaabun mawdu'ah.

15. Wa namaariqu masfoofah.

16. Wa zarabiy yu mab thoothah.

17. Afalaa yandhuruna elaal ibili kaiyfa khuliqat.

18. Wa elas samaa-i kaiyfa rufi'at.

19. Wa elaal jibaali kaiyfa nusibat.

20. Wa elaal -ardi kaiyfa sutihat.

21. Fa dhak kir innamaa anta mudhak kir.

22. Lasta 'alayhim be musaiytir.

23. Illaa man tawallaa wa kafar.

24. Fa yu 'adh dhebuhul lahul 'adhaabal akbar.

25. Inna elaynaa eyabahoom.

26. Thoomma inna 'alaynaa hisaabahum.

The Dawn
89 Al Fajr
Early Meccan Period

🔍 <u>BACKGROUND</u>

The message of this chapter is to tell the leaders of Mecca that they had better stop trying to fight against Allah. If they don't stop worshipping idols and being bad, then Allah will destroy them like the ancient people of the past. At this time, the idol-worshippers were hurting innocent Muslims, so this chapter is telling them to watch out.

In the Name of Allah,
the Compassionate, the Merciful

By the dawn, * by the ten (sacred) nights (of Hajj), * by the even and the odd, * and by the cycle of night and its passing, * for those who have sense is there any evidence more convincing than this? [1-5]

Don't you see how your Lord dealt with the people of 'Ad * from (the city of) Iram, of the tall towers − * (a city) unlike any other built in the land? * And with the (people of) Thamud, (who lived in cities) made of cut rock? [6-9]

And what of Pharaoh, master of legions? * All of them acted like tyrants in the land * and caused so much chaos and disorder. [10-12]

And so your Lord (brought them down) with terrible disasters, * for your Lord is always watchful. [13-14]

Now as for (the average) person, whenever his Lord generously tests him through honor and good times, he says, *"Even My Lord is good to me!"* [15]

Yet, whenever he's tested by having his resources held back, he cries, *"Even My Lord is against me!"* [16]

Not so! There's no way (you can blame Allah for your troubles,) when you're not even generous with orphans, * nor do you tell each other to feed the poor. [17-18]

You waste your inheritance eagerly, * and on top of that you want wealth more than anything else! [19-20]

But no! When the earth is ground to powder * and your Lord comes with hosts of angels in ranks, * and when Hellfire will be brought very close on that day, then on that day, (every) person will realize (what he's done), but how will it help him then? [21-23]

(In shame) he will cry, *"Oh, the misfortune! If only I would have sent some (good deeds) ahead (to prepare) for this (new) life!"* [24]

On that day, no one will punish like Allah will punish, * and no one will tie-up like He will tie-up. [25-26]

"O soul at rest," (the good people will be told), * *"return to your Lord in satisfaction, even as (He is) completely satisfied with you. * Then enter now, and be among My servants. * Enter now into My Garden."* [27-30]

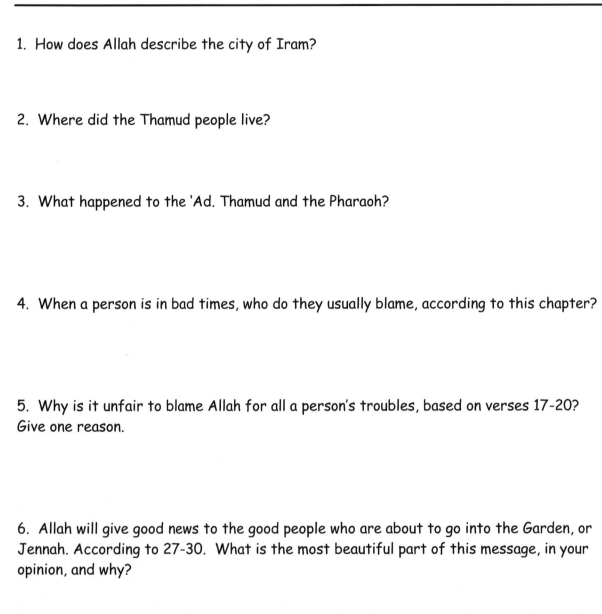

Think About It

1. How does Allah describe the city of Iram?

2. Where did the Thamud people live?

3. What happened to the 'Ad. Thamud and the Pharaoh?

4. When a person is in bad times, who do they usually blame, according to this chapter?

5. Why is it unfair to blame Allah for all a person's troubles, based on verses 17-20? Give one reason.

6. Allah will give good news to the good people who are about to go into the Garden, or Jennah. According to 27-30. What is the most beautiful part of this message, in your opinion, and why?

بِسْمِ اللهِ الرَّحْمَنِ الرَّحِيمِ

وَالْفَجْرِ ۝١

وَلَيَالٍ عَشْرٍ ۝٢

وَّالشَّفْعِ وَالْوَتْرِ ۝٣

وَالَّيْلِ اِذَا يَسْرِ ۝٤

هَلْ فِيْ ذَلِكَ قَسَمٌ لِّذِيْ حِجْرٍ ۝٥

اَلَمْ تَرَ كَيْفَ فَعَلَ رَبُّكَ بِعَادٍ ۝٦

اِرَمَ ذَاتِ الْعِمَادِ ۝٧

الَّتِيْ لَمْ يُخْلَقْ مِثْلُهَا فِي الْبِلَادِ ۝٨

وَثَمُوْدَ الَّذِيْنَ جَابُوا الصَّخْرَ بِالْوَادِ ۝٩

وَفِرْعَوْنَ ذِى الْاَوْتَادِ ۝١٠

الَّذِيْنَ طَغَوْا فِي الْبِلَادِ ۝١١

فَاَكْثَرُوْا فِيْهَا الْفَسَادَ ۝١٢

فَصَبَّ عَلَيْهِمْ رَبُّكَ سَوْطَ عَذَابٍ ۝

إِنَّ رَبَّكَ لَبِالْمِرْصَادِ ۝

فَأَمَّا الْإِنْسَانُ إِذَا مَا ابْتَلَاهُ رَبُّهُ فَأَكْرَمَهُ
وَنَعَّمَهُ فَيَقُولُ رَبِّي أَكْرَمَنِ ۝

وَأَمَّا إِذَا مَا ابْتَلَاهُ فَقَدَرَ عَلَيْهِ رِزْقَهُ
فَيَقُولُ رَبِّي أَهَانَنِ ۝

كَلَّا بَلْ لَّا تُكْرِمُونَ الْيَتِيمَ ۝

وَلَا تَحَاضُّونَ عَلَى طَعَامِ الْمِسْكِينِ ۝

وَتَأْكُلُونَ التُّرَاثَ أَكْلًا لَّمًّا ۝

وَّتُحِبُّونَ الْمَالَ حُبًّا جَمًّا ۝

كَلَّا إِذَا دُكَّتِ الْأَرْضُ دَكًّا دَكًّا ۝

وَّجَاءَ رَبُّكَ وَالْمَلَكُ صَفًّا صَفًّا ۝

وَجِائْءَ يَوْمَئِذٍ بِجَهَنَّمَ ۚ يَوْمَئِذٍ يَّتَذَكَّرُ الْإِنْسَانُ وَأَنَّى لَهُ الذِّكْرَى ۝

يَقُولُ يٰلَيْتَنِي قَدَّمْتُ لِحَيَاتِي ۝

فَيَوْمَئِذٍ لَّا يُعَذِّبُ عَذَابَهُ أَحَدٌ ۝

وَّلَا يُوثِقُ وَثَاقَهُ أَحَدٌ ۝

يَا أَيَّتُهَا النَّفْسُ الْمُطْمَئِنَّةُ ۝

ارْجِعِي إِلَى رَبِّكِ رَاضِيَةً مَّرْضِيَّةً ۝

فَادْخُلِي فِي عِبَادِي ۝

وَادْخُلِي جَنَّتِي ۝

Surah 89 Transliteration

Bismillahir Rahmanir Rahim

1. Wal fajr.

2. Wa layaalin 'ashr.

3. Wash shaf'e wal watr.

4. Wal layle edhaa yasr.

5. Hal fee dhaalika qasamulidhe hijr?

6. A lam tara kaiyfa fa'ala rabbuka be 'aad?

7. Irama dhaatil 'emaad.

8. Allate lam yukhlaq mithluhaa fil bilaad.

9. Wa thamood al ladheena jaaboos sakhra bil waad?

10. Wa Fir'aowna dhil owtaad?

11. Alladheena taghaw fil bilaad.

12. Fa ak tharoo feehaal fasaad.

13. Fa sabba 'alayhim rabbuka sowta 'adhaab.

14. Inna rabbaka labil mirsawd.

15. Fa ammaal insaanu edhaa maab talaahu rabbuhu fa ak ramahu wa na'amahu fa yaqoolu rabbee ak raman.

16. Wa ammaa edhaa maab talaahu fa qadara 'alayhe rizqahu fa yaqoolu rabbee ahaanan.

17. Kallaa bal laa tukrimoonal yateem.

18. Wa laa tahaad doona 'alaa taw'aamil miskeen.

19. Wa ta-kulunat turaatha aklal lammaa.

20. Wa tuhib boonal maala hubban jammaa.

21. Kallaa edha duk katil -ardu dakkan dakka.

22. Wa jaa-a rabbuka wal malaku saffan saffa.

23. Wa jee-a yowma -edhin be jahannama yowma -edhin yatadhak karul insaanu wa annaa lahudh dhikraa.

24. Yaqoolu yaa laytanee qad damtu le hayaatee.

25. Fa yowma -edhil laa yu'adh dhebu 'adhaabahu ahad.

26. Wa laa yoothiqu wathaaqahu ahad.

27. Ya aiy yatuhaan nafsul mutma-innah.

28. Irji 'ee elaa rabbiki radiyatan mardiyyah.

29. Fad khulee fee 'ebaadee.

30. Wad khulee jannatee.

The Land
90 Al Balad
Early Meccan Period

🔍 BACKGROUND

The people of Mecca loved their traditions. They worshipped idols and followed a lot of bad customs. They did not want anyone to tell them to change for the better. Most of the Meccan leaders decided that people should not listen to the Prophet. Then they started bothering him and hurting his followers.

This chapter was revealed to the Prophet to let them know that Allah was watching them. He knew they were bad people, and this chapter tells them that there is another and better road to take in life. If they would only listen!

*In the Name of Allah,
the Compassionate, the Merciful*

I promise by this land, and you Muhammad are from this land, and I promise by the link between a parent and a child that We have made each person to work hard *in this world*. [1-4]

Does he think that there is no one stronger than him? He says, "*I have so much money, I can even waste it!*" But does he think no one is watching him? [5-7]

Didn't We give him a pair of eyes, a tongue and a pair of lips and then showed to him the two roads *of good and evil*? [8-10]

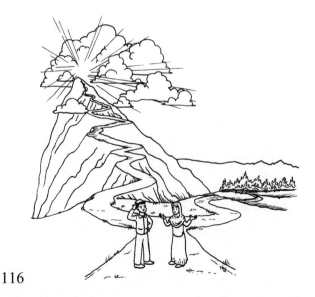

116

Yet, he does not even try to go on the harder road, and how can you understand what the harder road is? [11-12]

It is to give freedom to a slave, or to feed, on a hungry day, family members who lost their parents or to feed the poor person who is lying in the dust. [13-16]

If a person does all that then he will be with the believers who teach each other patience and kindness. Those are the companions of the right side. [17-18]

But those who try to cover over Our revealed verses are the companions of the left side. They will have fire falling all over them from everywhere. [19-20]

117

☁ Think About It

1. Why do you think that verses 1-4 say that people were born to work hard? Give an example of hard work in our lives.

2. If a person never wants to work hard and always wants to take the easy road, what do people say about a person like that and why?

3. What is the difference between the harder road of life and the easier road, according to this chapter?

4. Verses 13-16 give examples of righteous deeds. In the box below, draw a picture of a good deed in action.

بِسْمِ اللهِ الرَّحْمٰنِ الرَّحِيْمِ

لَآ أُقْسِمُ بِهٰذَا الْبَلَدِ ۝

وَأَنْتَ حِلٌّ بِهٰذَا الْبَلَدِ ۝

وَوَالِدٍ وَّمَا وَلَدَ ۝

لَقَدْ خَلَقْنَا الْإِنْسَانَ فِيْ كَبَدٍ ۝

أَيَحْسَبُ أَنْ لَّنْ يَّقْدِرَ عَلَيْهِ أَحَدٌ ۝

يَقُوْلُ أَهْلَكْتُ مَالًا لُّبَدًا ۝

أَيَحْسَبُ أَنْ لَّمْ يَرَهُ أَحَدٌ ۝

أَلَمْ نَجْعَلْ لَّهُ عَيْنَيْنِ ۝

وَلِسَانًا وَّشَفَتَيْنِ ۝

وَهَدَيْنٰهُ النَّجْدَيْنِ ۝

فَلَا اقْتَحَمَ الْعَقَبَةَ ۝

وَمَآ أَدْرٰىكَ مَا الْعَقَبَةُ ۝

فَكُّ رَقَبَةٍ ۙ ۞

اَوْ اِطْعَامٌ فِیْ یَوْمٍ ذِیْ مَسْغَبَةٍ ۙ ۞

یَّتِیْمًا ذَا مَقْرَبَةٍ ۙ ۞

اَوْ مِسْکِیْنًا ذَا مَتْرَبَةٍ ؕ ۞

ثُمَّ کَانَ مِنَ الَّذِیْنَ اٰمَنُوْا وَ تَوَاصَوْا

بِالصَّبْرِ وَ تَوَاصَوْا بِالْمَرْحَمَةِ ؕ ۞

اُولٰٓئِکَ اَصْحٰبُ الْمَیْمَنَةِ ؕ ۞

وَ الَّذِیْنَ کَفَرُوْا بِاٰیٰتِنَا هُمْ اَصْحٰبُ الْمَشْـَٔمَةِ ؕ ۞

عَلَیْهِمْ نَارٌ مُّؤْصَدَةٌ ۞

Surah 90 Transliteration

Bismillahir Rahmanir Rahim

1. Laa ooq simu be haadhal balad.

2. Wa anta hil lun be haadhal balad.

3. Wa waalidin wa maa walad.

4. Laqad khalaqnaal insaana fee kabad.

5. Ayah sabu al laiy yaqdira 'alayhe ahad.

6. Yaqoolu ahlaktu maalal lubadaa.

7. Ayah sabu al lam yarahu ahad.

8. Alam naj'al lahu 'aiynaiyn.

9. Wa lisaanawn wa shafataiyn.

10. Wa hadaiy naahun najdaiyn.

11. Falaaq tahamal 'aqabah.

12. Wa maa ad raaka maal 'aqabah?

13. Fak ku raqabah.

14. Ow it'awmun fee yowmin dhee masghabah.

15. Yateemaan dha maqrabah.

16. Ow miskeenaan dha matrabah.

17. Thoomma kaana minal ladheena aamanoo wa tawaasow bis sabre wa tawaasow bil marhamah.

18. Oola-ika as haabul maiymanah.

19. Wal ladheena kafaroo be aayaatinaa hoom as haabul mash-amah.

20. 'Alayhim naarun mu-sawdah.

The Sun
91 Ash-Shamms
Early Meccan Period

Q BACKGROUND

The idol-worshippers of Mecca started to bother the Prophet around the time that this chapter was revealed. They did not like to hear that there was only One God. They wanted to keep on worshipping their many idols made of stone and wood. This chapter asks them to remember an older civilization that disobeyed Allah. If they were bad, then they might also suffer the same end.

In the Name of Allah,
the Compassionate, the Merciful

By the sun and its radiance, * by the moon as it trails along, * by the day as it brightens, * by the night as it covers up, * by the sky and what built it, * by the earth and its wide expanse, * and by the soul and its balanced (nature) * and its built-in knowledge (of right and wrong) - [1-8]

(By these tokens, know that) the one who makes his soul pure will be successful, * while the one who makes it dirty will fail. [9-10]

The (people of) Thamud rejected (this truth) in their arrogance. * The worst man among them stood up (and volunteered to do an evil deed). [11-12]

Their messenger from Allah had told them, "*This camel belongs to Allah, so let her drink (at the wells).*" [13]

Then they called him a pretender, and (the bad man) cruelly cut her.

Because of that, their Lord destroyed all of them equally for their crimes, * and He is not afraid of what He does. [14-15]

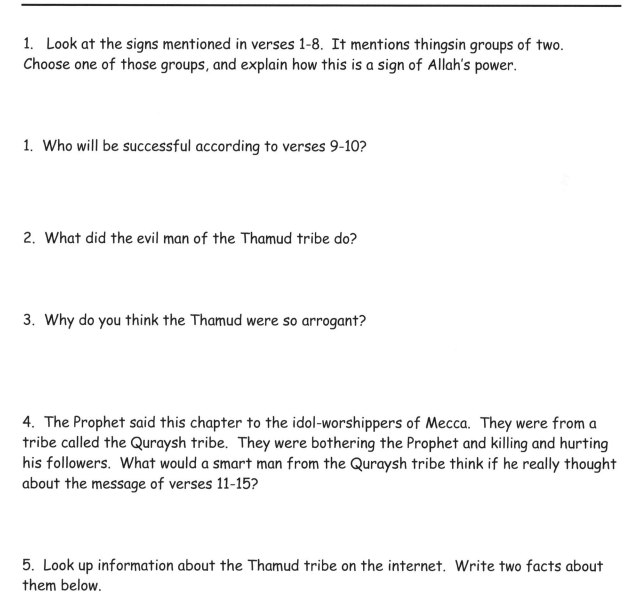

Think About It

1. Look at the signs mentioned in verses 1-8. It mentions things in groups of two. Choose one of those groups, and explain how this is a sign of Allah's power.

1. Who will be successful according to verses 9-10?

2. What did the evil man of the Thamud tribe do?

3. Why do you think the Thamud were so arrogant?

4. The Prophet said this chapter to the idol-worshippers of Mecca. They were from a tribe called the Quraysh tribe. They were bothering the Prophet and killing and hurting his followers. What would a smart man from the Quraysh tribe think if he really thought about the message of verses 11-15?

5. Look up information about the Thamud tribe on the internet. Write two facts about them below.

بِسْمِ اللهِ الرَّحْمٰنِ الرَّحِيمِ

وَالشَّمْسِ وَضُحٰىهَا ۝١

وَالْقَمَرِ إِذَا تَلٰىهَا ۝٢

وَالنَّهَارِ إِذَا جَلّٰىهَا ۝٣

وَالَّيْلِ إِذَا يَغْشٰىهَا ۝٤

وَالسَّمَآءِ وَمَا بَنٰىهَا ۝٥

وَالْاَرْضِ وَمَا طَحٰىهَا ۝٦

وَنَفْسٍ وَّمَا سَوّٰىهَا ۝٧

فَاَلْهَمَهَا فُجُوْرَهَا وَتَقْوٰىهَا ۝٨

قَدْ اَفْلَحَ مَنْ زَكّٰىهَا ۝٩

وَقَدْ خَابَ مَنْ دَسّٰىهَا ۝١٠

كَذَّبَتْ ثَمُوْدُ بِطَغْوٰىهَآ ۝١١

126

إِذِ انْبَعَثَ أَشْقَىٰهَا ۝

فَقَالَ لَهُمْ رَسُولُ اللَّهِ نَاقَةَ اللَّهِ وَسُقْيَٰهَا ۝

فَكَذَّبُوهُ فَعَقَرُوهَا فَدَمْدَمَ عَلَيْهِمْ رَبُّهُم بِذَنْبِهِمْ فَسَوَّىٰهَا ۝

وَلَا يَخَافُ عُقْبَٰهَا ۝

Surah 91 Transliteration

Bismillahir Rahmanir Rahim

1. Wash shammsi wa duhaa haa.

2. Wal qamari edhaa talaa haa.

3. Wan nahaari edhaa jallaa haa.

4. Wal layle edhaa yagh shaa haa.

5. Was samaa-i wa maa banaa haa.

6. Wal -ardi wa maa tahaa haa.

7. Wa nafsin wa maa sawwaa haa.

8. Fa al hamahaa fujoorahaa wa taqwaa haa.

9. Qad aflaha man zak kaa haa.

10. Wa qad khawba man dassaa haa.

11. Kadh dhabat thamoodu be taghwaa haa.

12. Edhin ba'athaa ashqawhaa.

13. Fa qawla lahoom rasoolul lahe naaqatal lahi wa suqyaa haa.

14. Fakadh dhaboohu fa 'aqaruhaa fa damdama 'alayhim rabbuhoom be dhambehim fasawwaa haa.

15. Wa laa yakhawfu 'ooqbaa haa.

The Night
92 Al-Layl
Early Meccan Period

Q BACKGROUND

This chapter was revealed so the Prophet could teach people that they have to be active in being good and right. Collecting money all the time will fill the empty place in a person's heart. Only Allah can save us from being greedy and small in our thinking.

In the Name of Allah,
the Compassionate, the Merciful

By the cover of night, * by the day as it shines bright, * and by the creation of male and female, * truly, different are the goals (for which you work). [1-4]

And so for the one who gives (in charity), keeps himself (from evil), * and who promotes goodness, * We'll smooth (his path) to an easy end. [5-7]

For the greedy miser who thinks he doesn't need anything * and who doesn't care about goodness, * We'll smooth (his path) to a horrible end. * What will all his money do for him as he goes down (into the pit of Hell)? [8-11]

Indeed, We've taken it upon Ourselves to provide guidance, * because the end and the beginning (of all things) belongs to Us. [12-13]

So now, I'm warning you of a burning fire * that no one will enter but the most horrible (of all people), * those who deny (the truth) and turn away. [14-16]

Charity for the Sake of Allah

🔍 BACKGROUND

It is said that verses 17-21 were revealed about Abu Bakr who bought the freedom of seven convert slaves from the idol-worshippers, including one man named Bilal ibn Rabah.

The idol-worshippers began saying that Abu Bakr did it only as a favor for Bilal, who suffered great torture at the hands of his master, and this section makes the point that Abu Bakr did what he did only for Allah's sake. (al-Itqān)

The one who was mindful (of his duty to Allah), however, will be far away from it. * That kind of person purified his money (through charity) * and he gave no thought to being repaid with favors. [17-19]

His only concern was seeking the approval of his Lord, the Most High. * Soon, he will have the greatest happiness! [20-21]

130

☁ Think About It

1. Look at verses 1-4. How does Allah use pairs when talking about our goals in life?

2. The path of being good in this world means self-control and sharing. This is hard, but if we do that, what does Allah tell us our ultimate destiny will be like in verses 5-7?

3. Look at verses 8-11. Choose one of the qualities of a bad person and explain what it is and what makes it so bad to be like that.

4. Why do you think Allah is warning us to stay away from bad deeds so much?

5. Some people make the focus of their lives only about making money and getting rich. Islam does not forbid people from making maoney, or being rich, but it does tell us to be careful about some things as we are making money. What is something Islam asks us to remember when it comes to money and gaining it.

6. What did the idol-worshippers say about Abu Bakr and the reasons for his charity?

7. How do we 'purify' our wealth and money? Give an example also.

بِسْمِ اللهِ الرَّحْمٰنِ الرَّحِيمِ

وَالَّيْلِ إِذَا يَغْشٰى ۝١

وَالنَّهَارِ إِذَا تَجَلّٰى ۝٢

وَمَا خَلَقَ الذَّكَرَ وَالْاُنْثٰى ۝٣

اِنَّ سَعْيَكُمْ لَشَتّٰى ۝٤

فَاَمَّا مَنْ اَعْطٰى وَاتَّقٰى ۝٥

وَصَدَّقَ بِالْحُسْنٰى ۝٦

فَسَنُيَسِّرُهُ لِلْيُسْرٰى ۝٧

وَاَمَّا مَنْ بَخِلَ وَاسْتَغْنٰى ۝٨

وَكَذَّبَ بِالْحُسْنٰى ۝٩

فَسَنُيَسِّرُهُ لِلْعُسْرٰى ۝١٠

وَمَا يُغْنِي عَنْهُ مَالُهُ إِذَا تَرَدّٰى ۝١١

اِنَّ عَلَيْنَا لَلْهُدٰى ۝١٢

وَاِنَّ لَنَا لَلْاٰخِرَةَ وَالْاُوْلٰى ۝١٣

فَأَنْذَرْتُكُمْ نَارًا تَلَظَّى ﴿١٤﴾

لَا يَصْلَاهَآ إِلَّا الْأَشْقَى ﴿١٥﴾

الَّذِى كَذَّبَ وَتَوَلَّى ﴿١٦﴾

وَسَيُجَنَّبُهَا الْأَتْقَى ﴿١٧﴾

الَّذِى يُؤْتِى مَالَهُ يَتَزَكَّى ﴿١٨﴾

وَمَا لِأَحَدٍ عِنْدَهُ مِنْ نِعْمَةٍ تُجْزَى ﴿١٩﴾

إِلَّا ابْتِغَآءَ وَجْهِ رَبِّهِ الْأَعْلَى ﴿٢٠﴾

وَلَسَوْفَ يَرْضَى ﴿٢١﴾

Surah 92 Transliteration

Bismillahir Rahmanir Rahim

1. Wal layle edhaa yagh shaa.

2. Waan nahaari edhaa tajallaa.

3. Wa maa khalaqadh dhakara wal oonthaa.

4. Inna sa'yakoom lashataa.

5. Fa ammaa man 'atawat taqaw.

6. Wa saddaqa bil husnaa.

7. Fasa nuyassiruhu lil yusraa.

8. Wa ammaa man bakhila wa staghnaa.

9. Wa kadh dhaba bil husnaa.

10. Fasa nuyassiruhu lil 'oosraa.

11. Wa maa yughnee 'anhu maaluhu edhaa tarad daa.

12. Inna 'alaynaa lal hudaa.

13. Wa inna lanaa lal aakhirata wal oola.

14. Fa an dhar tukoom naaraan taladh dhaa.

15. Laa yaslaahaa illaal ashqaw.

16. Alladhee kadh dhaba wa tawallaa.

17. Wa sayujan nabuhal atqaw.

18. Alladhee yu-tee maalahu yatazak kaa.

19. Wa maa le ahadin 'indahu min ni'matin tooj zaa.

20. Illaab tighaw-a wajhi rabbihil 'alaa.

21. Wa lasowfa yardaw.

The Early Dawn

93 Ad-Duhā
Early Meccan Period

🔍 BACKGROUND

The Prophet had been getting messages from Angel Jibra'il for a few months, but then the messages suddenly stopped for a few months. The Prophet started to feel real bad about it. He thought he might have made Allah angry with him. That's why this chapter opens with the words that say allah was not angry with him.

*In the Name of Allah,
the Compassionate, the Merciful*

By the light of daybreak * and by the still of the night, * your Lord has not left you, (Muhammad,) nor is He angry. [1-3]

Your future is brighter than your present time, * because your Lord will soon grant you (what you really want), and you will be very happy. [4-5]

Didn't He find you an orphan and shelter you? * Didn't He find you lost and show you the way? * Didn't He find you in need and make you independent? [6-8]

And so don't be mean to the orphan * nor ignore the requests (of the poor), * and continue to declare (the mercy) and blessings of your Lord. [9-11]

🗯 Think About It

1. Why did the Prophet start to feel sad for a while?

2. Write down the three ways that Allah said that He helped the Prophet overcome his challenges in life, based on verses 6-8.

     A.

     B.

     C.

3. Think of a time in your life, or in the life of someone you know, when they had a big problem or challenge, but then they were helped out of nowhere, either by a person, or learning something new inside that helped them to deal with the issue. What is the help the came to them?

4. When some bad thing happens, we should ask Allah to help us. There is a du'a for that. Read the du'a below and memorize it.

إنَّا لله وَإنَا إلَيْهِ راجِعون ، اللهُمَّ أجُرْني في مُصيبَتي، واخْلُفْ لي خَيْراً مِنْها.

"We are from Allah, and to Him we will return. O Allah save me from my problem and bring to me, after it something better." *(Sahih Muslim)*

"'Innaa lillaahi wa 'innaa 'ilayhi raaji'oon, Allaahumma'-jurni fee museebatee wa 'akhliflee khayran minhaa."

بِسْمِ اللَّهِ الرَّحْمَنِ الرَّحِيمِ

وَالضُّحَى ۝١

وَالَّيْلِ إِذَا سَجَى ۝٢

مَا وَدَّعَكَ رَبُّكَ وَمَا قَلَى ۝٣

وَلَلْآخِرَةُ خَيْرٌ لَّكَ مِنَ الْأُولَى ۝٤

وَلَسَوْفَ يُعْطِيكَ رَبُّكَ فَتَرْضَى ۝٥

أَلَمْ يَجِدْكَ يَتِيمًا فَآوَى ۝٦

وَوَجَدَكَ ضَالًّا فَهَدَى ۝٧

وَوَجَدَكَ عَائِلًا فَأَغْنَى ۝٨

فَأَمَّا الْيَتِيمَ فَلَا تَقْهَرْ ۝٩

وَأَمَّا السَّائِلَ فَلَا تَنْهَرْ ۝١٠

وَأَمَّا بِنِعْمَةِ رَبِّكَ فَحَدِّثْ ۝١١

Surah 93 Transliteration

Bismillahir Rahmanir Rahim

1. Wad Duhaa.

2. Wal layle edhaa sajaa.

3. Maa wad da'aka rabbuka wa maa qawlaa.

4. Wa lal aakhiratu khaiyrul laka minal oola.

5. Wa lasowfa yu' teeka rabbuka fa tardaw.

6. A lem yajidka yateemaan faa aawaa.

7. Wa wajadaka daawllan fahadaa.

8. Wa wajadaka 'aa-elaan fa aghnaa.

9. Fa ammaal yateema fa laa taqhar.

10. Wa ammaas saa-ela fa laa tanhar.

11. Wa ammaa be ni'mati rabbika fa haddeth.

The Broadening
94 Ash-Sharh
Early Meccan Period

🔍 BACKGROUND

This chapter was revealed after chapter 93. It continues the same basic message from that chapter, that Allah has been helping the Prophet and will make his struggle successful.

In the Name of Allah,
the Compassionate, the Merciful

(Muhammad,) didn't We increase your understanding * and free you of the burden (of worry) * that weighed heavily upon your back? * (Didn't We) raise your reputation, as well? [1-4]

And so it is that every bad time has its better time. * (No matter what), bad times are followed by better times. *

And so even when you're free (from all your other jobs), stay firm (on the path), * and turn yourself towards your Lord (with a focused mind). [5-8]

 **Think About It**

1. The Prophet was full of worry in the early days of his mission. He was scared about not being believed. He didn't know why he was chosen. The revelations were new to him, and he never would have imagined his life would be changed in so many ways. Looking at the message of this surah, in what way does Allah reassure him that he will be supported and successful?

2. When the Prophet was preaching and gaining converts, he had so many jobs and duties to teach, help people and deal with problems the idol worshippers were causing, but there were quiet times when he had some time to himself. What does this surah tell him about those times?

3. People often talk about good times and bands times, and how one follows the other. Think about the different times you learned about in history or social studies classes. Choose one of those topics, when there were bad times, but then good times followed. Explain the situation in one paragraph below.

بِسْمِ اللهِ الرَّحْمٰنِ الرَّحِيمِ

اَلَمْ نَشْرَحْ لَكَ صَدْرَكَ ۝١

وَوَضَعْنَا عَنْكَ وِزْرَكَ ۝٢

اَلَّذِيٓ اَنْقَضَ ظَهْرَكَ ۝٣

وَرَفَعْنَا لَكَ ذِكْرَكَ ۝٤

فَاِنَّ مَعَ الْعُسْرِ يُسْرًا ۝٥

اِنَّ مَعَ الْعُسْرِ يُسْرًا ۝٦

فَاِذَا فَرَغْتَ فَانْصَبْ ۝٧

وَاِلٰى رَبِّكَ فَارْغَبْ ۝٨

Surah 94 Transliteration

Bismillahir Rahmanir Rahim

1. A lem nashrah laka sadrak.

2. Wa wada'naa 'anka wizrak.

3. Alladhee anqada dhah rak.

4. Wa rafa'naa laka dhikrak.

5. Fa inna ma'al 'oosri yusraa.

6. Inna ma'al 'oosri yusraa.

7. Fa edhaa faraghta fan sab.

8. Wa elaa rabbika far ghab.

The Fig
95 At-Teen
Early Meccan Period

BACKGROUND

This chapter is about how people are responsible for their own actions. The idol-worshippers in Mecca did not care if they were good or bad. Their idols of wood and stone did not ask them to be good. Their idols could not even tell them what they wanted them to do! The symbols mentioned in the beginning are references to important places and prophets of the past.

In the Name of Allah,
the Compassionate, the Merciful

By the fig and the olive, * by the Mountain of Tur, * and by this city secure, * so it is that We've created the human being in the best form. [1-4]

Then We bring him down to the lowest of the low * - all except for those who believe and do what's good and right. For them is a reward that will never end. [5-6]

So how can (the coming) judgment be denied? * Isn't Allah the most fit to decide? [7-8]

☁ Think About It

1. What do you think it means that human beings were created in the best form?

2. How do people ruin the beautiful life that Allah created for us?

3. In the box below, draw pictures of all the four symbols mentioned in the opening of this chapter. (A fig, an olive, a mountain and a small city.)

بِسْمِ اللهِ الرَّحْمَنِ الرَّحِيمِ

وَالتِّينِ وَالزَّيْتُونِ ۝

وَطُورِ سِينِينَ ۝

وَهَذَا الْبَلَدِ الْأَمِينِ ۝

لَقَدْ خَلَقْنَا الْإِنْسَانَ فِي أَحْسَنِ تَقْوِيمٍ ۝

ثُمَّ رَدَدْنَاهُ أَسْفَلَ سَافِلِينَ ۝

إِلَّا الَّذِينَ آمَنُوا وَعَمِلُوا الصَّالِحَاتِ

فَلَهُمْ أَجْرٌ غَيْرُ مَمْنُونٍ ۝

فَمَا يُكَذِّبُكَ بَعْدُ بِالدِّينِ ۝

أَلَيْسَ اللهُ بِأَحْكَمِ الْحَاكِمِينَ ۝

Surah 95 Transliteration

Bismillahir Rahmanir Rahim

1. Wat teeni waz zaytoon.

2. Wa toori see neen.

3. Wa haadhal baladil ameen.

4. Laqad khalaqnaal insaana fee ah sani taqweem.

5. Thoomma radadnaahu asfala saafileen.

6. Illal ladheena aamanoo wa 'amiloos sawlihaati fa lahoom ajrun ghairu mamnoon.

7. Fa maa yukadh dhibuka ba'du bid deen.

8. A laysal lahu be ahkamil hakimeen?

The Clinging Thing
96 Al 'Alaq
Early Meccan Period

🔍 BACKGROUND

This chapter has the very first verses that were given to the Prophet. He was alone in a cave to think and pray when an invisible angel came and told him to read. Muhammad was scared and all he could say was that he did not know how to read.

The unseen angel squeezed him from all sides with its power and then told him to read again, and Muhammad repeated that he did not know how. After a third time of being squeezed real hard, Muhammad asked, "What do you want me to read?"

Then verses 1 to 5 were given to him. After that, Muhammad ran home to his wife and he was very scared because he did not know what happened to him.

In the Name of Allah,
the Compassionate, the Merciful

Read in the name of your Lord Who created - * Who created people from a hanging thing *in the womb*. * Read, because your Lord is very Generous. [1-3]

He taught people *how to write* with the **pen**. *

He *used writing* to teach people what they didn't know before. [4-5]

But still people go against following *the truth*. * They even think that they can take care of things *all by themselves*, * but everything will go back to Allah! [6-8]

148

🔍 BACKGROUND

The Prophet's Uncle, Abu Jahl, was always trying to bother the Prophet when he prayed near the Ka'bah.

Abu Jahl said, "By the gods, if I ever catch him praying, I will set my foot on his neck and rub his face in the dust."

This next group of verses were revealed to the Prophet about Abu Jahl - and others like him - who try to stop people from praying to Allah. (Ahmed, Tirmidhi, Nisa'i)

Have you ever seen the one who tries to stop * a servant *of Allah* from praying? * Do you (think) that he is doing the most proper thing * or that he even **cares** (about Allah)? [9-12]

Do you see that he is he really covering over *the truth* and turning *his head away? * Doesn't he know that Allah **sees** him?* [13-14]

Let him be warned then, that unless he changes his ways, We will drag him down by the hair of his forehead - * *his lying, sinful forehead!* [15-16]

Then let him call upon his supporters (for help), * and then We will also make a call, *but to the forces of punishment!* [17-18]

No way! Don't let yourself get **side-tracked** by someone like that. Instead, bow down *in prayer* and come closer *to Allah.* [19]

149

Think About It

1. Why do you think the invention of writing is so important?

2. What bad thing did Abu Jahl want to do to the Prophet?

3. What does Allah say about people in verses 6-8?

4. Imagine the scene on Judgment Day, when a person who was evil and arrogant in this life is on their knees in fear as they realize the truth of all their evil. What is one thing you could say to them to help them understand how wrong they were in the world?

Fill in the Words on the lines below.
Look at the **BOLD** words in the main text to see where they go

Words to Use

Side-tracked   Sees   Cares   Pen

---

1. Do you think he is doing the most proper thing or that he even _____ about Allah?

2. Don't let yourself get _____ by someone like that.

3. He taught *people how to write* with the _____.

4. *Doesn't he know that Allah _____ him?*

بِسْمِ اللهِ الرَّحْمٰنِ الرَّحِيْمِ

اِقْرَأْ بِاسْمِ رَبِّكَ الَّذِىْ خَلَقَ ۝١

خَلَقَ الْاِنْسَانَ مِنْ عَلَقٍ ۝٢

اِقْرَأْ وَرَبُّكَ الْاَكْرَمُ ۝٣

الَّذِىْ عَلَّمَ بِالْقَلَمِ ۝٤

عَلَّمَ الْاِنْسَانَ مَا لَمْ يَعْلَمْ ۝٥

كَلَّا اِنَّ الْاِنْسَانَ لَيَطْغٰى ۝٦

اَنْ رَّاٰهُ اسْتَغْنٰى ۝٧

اِنَّ اِلٰى رَبِّكَ الرُّجْعٰى ۝٨

اَرَءَيْتَ الَّذِىْ يَنْهٰى ۝٩

عَبْدًا اِذَا صَلّٰى ۝١٠

151

اَرَءَيْتَ اِنْ كَانَ عَلَى الْهُدٰى ۞ ﴿١١﴾

اَوْ اَمَرَ بِالتَّقْوٰى ۞ ﴿١٢﴾

اَرَءَيْتَ اِنْ كَذَّبَ وَتَوَلّٰى ۞ ﴿١٣﴾

اَلَمْ يَعْلَمْ بِاَنَّ اللّٰهَ يَرٰى ۞ ﴿١٤﴾

كَلَّا لَئِنْ لَّمْ يَنْتَهِ ۙ لَنَسْفَعًۢا بِالنَّاصِيَةِ ۞ ﴿١٥﴾

نَاصِيَةٍ كَاذِبَةٍ خَاطِئَةٍ ۞ ﴿١٦﴾

فَلْيَدْعُ نَادِيَهْ ۞ ﴿١٧﴾

سَنَدْعُ الزَّبَانِيَةَ ۞ ﴿١٨﴾

كَلَّا ۖ لَا تُطِعْهُ وَاسْجُدْ وَاقْتَرِبْ ۩ ﴿١٩﴾

152

Surah 96 Transliteration

Bismillahir Rahmanir Rahim

1. Iqra- bismi rabbikal ladhee khalaq.

2. Khalaqal insaana min 'alaq.

3. Iqra- wa rabbukal akram.

4. Alladhee 'allama bil qalam.

5. 'Allamal insaana maa lam ya'lam.

6. Kallaa innal insaana layatghaw.

7. Ar ra ahus staghnaa.

8. Inna elaa rabbikar ruj'aa.

9. Ara aiytal ladhee yanhaa?

10. 'Abdan edhaa sawllaa?

11. Ara aiyta in kaana 'alaal hudaa?

12. Ow amara bit taqwaa?

13. Ara aiyta in kadh dhaba wa tawallaa?

14. A lam ya'lam be annal laha yaraa?

15. Kallaa la-il lam yantahe lanasfa'aam bin naaseeyah.

16. Naasiyatin kaadh ebatin khawti-ah.

17. Fal yad'u naadeyah.

18. Sanad 'uz zabaaneyah.

19, Kallaa laa tuti'hu was jood waq tarib.   *

   *   (After reading the last line, face Mecca and bow down once in Sajda.)

Determination

97 Al Qadr
Early Meccan Period

🔍 BACKGROUND

Prophet Muhammad was resting in a cave in the month of Ramadan in the year 610. He went there to be alone to think and pray. Suddenly an angel came to him and told him that he was the new chosen prophet of Allah.

That special night is called *Laylatul Qadr*. That means *the Night of Measuring*. It is a special night that comes near the end of every Ramadan. It is the time when Allah sends down the angels with His commands for the year.

The Prophet said, "Whoever spends the night praying during the Night of Measuring, as a sign of his faith and seeking the reward of Allah, then all his previous sins will be forgiven." *(Bukhari)*

In the Name of Allah,
the Compassionate, the Merciful

For sure We *began* this revelation on the Night of Measuring, and how can you understand what the Night of Measuring is? [1-2]

The Night of Measuring is better than a thousand months, because the angels and the spirit *of Angel Jibra'il* come down, by their Lord's command, to finish every mission.

Peace is all around until the break of dawn! [3-5]

Think About It

1. The month of Ramadan is a time when Muslims think about their lives and promise to make changes to be better. Think of one good thing a person can do in his or her life to make it better. What is it?

2. Where was the Prophet when he got his first revelation from Allah?

3. How do you think he felt when the angel appeared?

4. What is one thing that happens on the night of Measuring?

5. Ask someone who has spent the night praying during Laylatul Qadr, or look for how someone on the internet described it. According to your source, how did the person feel afterwards, or what did they learn from it?

بِسْمِ اللهِ الرَّحْمٰنِ الرَّحِيْمِ

إِنَّآ أَنْزَلْنٰهُ فِيْ لَيْلَةِ الْقَدْرِ ۚ ﴿١﴾

وَمَآ أَدْرٰىكَ مَا لَيْلَةُ الْقَدْرِ ۚ ﴿٢﴾

لَيْلَةُ الْقَدْرِ ۙ خَيْرٌ مِّنْ أَلْفِ شَهْرٍ ۚ ﴿٣﴾

تَنَزَّلُ الْمَلٰٓئِكَةُ وَالرُّوْحُ فِيْهَا بِإِذْنِ رَبِّهِمْ ۚ

مِّنْ كُلِّ أَمْرٍ ۙ ﴿٤﴾

سَلٰمٌ ۛ هِيَ حَتّٰى مَطْلَعِ الْفَجْرِ ۛ ﴿٥﴾

Surah 97 Transliteration

Bismillahir Rahmanir Rahim

1. Innaa anzalnaahu fee laylatil qadr.

2. Wa maa ad raaka maa laylat ul qadr.

3. Laylatul qadri khaiyrun min alfi shahr.

4. Tanazzalul malaa-ekatu waar roohu feehaa be idhne rabbihim min kulle amr.

5. Salaamun heya hattaa mat la'il fajr.

The Clear Evidence
98 Al Bayyinah
Period Uncertain

🔍 BACKGROUND

When the Prophet read this chapter to one of his companions named Ubayy ibn Ka'b, he told Ubayy that Angel Jibrael ordered him to read it to him especially. Ubayy said, "O Messenger of Allah, was I mentioned by name?"

When the Prophet said, "Yes," Ubayy began to cry tears of joy. Then the Prophet said to him that Allah, Himself, said:

"If the son of Adam asked for a valley full of gold, and I gave it to him, then he would ask for a second. If he asked for a second one, and I gave it to him, then he would ask for a third."

"Nothing can fill his belly except dust," the Prophet sighed. "Allah accepts the repentance of one who turns to Him in repentance. The only way of life Allah accepts is the steady and true religion, not idol-worship, not Judaism nor Christianity, though whoever does good deeds, it shall not be for nothing." *(Ahmad)*

*In the Name of Allah,
the Compassionate, the Merciful*

Those who cover over *the truth* from among the Followers of Earlier Revelation and the idol-worshippers could not abandon *their mistaken ways* until clear proof *from Allah* was presented to them. [1]

That *proof was* a messenger from Allah who could read *to them* from holy pages that give clear and true teachings. [2-3]

But the Followers of Earlier Revelation didn't break up into groups until after *this kind of guidance* had already reached them before.

They did not follow it, even though they weren't taught anything more than to serve Allah, to be sincere to the religion that is His, and to start regular prayers and to give in charity. That's the straight way of life! [4-5]

For sure, those who cover *over the truth, now that it's come to them once more*, whether they're Followers of Earlier Revelation or idol-worshippers, have earned for themselves the fire of Hell, and they will stay in there *forever and ever.* They're the worst of all creatures! [6]

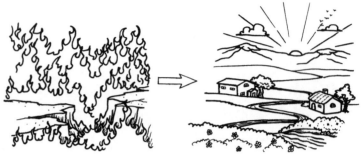

Now those who believe and do what's good and right are the best of creatures. Their reward is with their Lord: gardens that last forever with rivers flowing all around – and they will stay in there *forever and ever.*

Allah will be happy with them and they will be happy with Him. The person who loved his Lord will get *all of that!* [7-8]

☁ Think About It

1. Allah has sent many messages to people in the past. These messages were given to special people called prophets. Most people did not listen to their prophets, but after a long time the children or grandchildren accepted the messages. Of course, people like to argue about things, so after more time passed, people started to argue about their religion. Then they formed different groups that didn't like each other. That is why every religion has so many different groups. Doing this is bad because true religion wants to keep people together. Both Jews and Christians broke up into many different groups and some Muslims have done it also. This makes Allah angry. Why do you think it is wrong to break up into different groups and change the teachings of Allah?

2. Who are the Followers of Earlier Revelation? (Look in the introduction, last paragraph.)

3. How does Allah describe sincere religion? Write down two points from this surah.

4. Look up a diagram on the internet of either Christian, Jewish, Hindu, Buddhist or Muslim sects. Draw a picture that represents it's 3-10 major branches in the box below.

بِسْمِ اللهِ الرَّحْمٰنِ الرَّحِيْمِ

لَمْ يَكُنِ الَّذِيْنَ كَفَرُوْا مِنْ اَهْلِ الْكِتٰبِ وَالْمُشْرِكِيْنَ مُنْفَكِّيْنَ حَتّٰى تَأْتِيَهُمُ الْبَيِّنَةُ ۙ ١

رَسُوْلٌ مِّنَ اللهِ يَتْلُوْا صُحُفًا مُّطَهَّرَةً ۙ ٢

فِيْهَا كُتُبٌ قَيِّمَةٌ ۗ ٣

وَمَا تَفَرَّقَ الَّذِيْنَ اُوْتُوا الْكِتٰبَ اِلَّا مِنْ بَعْدِ مَا جَآءَتْهُمُ الْبَيِّنَةُ ۗ ٤

وَمَا اُمِرُوْٓا اِلَّا لِيَعْبُدُوا اللهَ مُخْلِصِيْنَ لَهُ الدِّيْنَ ۙ حُنَفَآءَ وَيُقِيْمُوا الصَّلٰوةَ وَيُؤْتُوا الزَّكٰوةَ وَذٰلِكَ دِيْنُ الْقَيِّمَةِ ۗ ٥

اِنَّ الَّذِيْنَ كَفَرُوْا مِنْ اَهْلِ الْكِتٰبِ وَالْمُشْرِكِيْنَ فِيْ نَارِ جَهَنَّمَ خٰلِدِيْنَ فِيْهَا ۗ اُولٰٓئِكَ هُمْ شَرُّ الْبَرِيَّةِ ۝

اِنَّ الَّذِيْنَ اٰمَنُوْا وَعَمِلُوا الصّٰلِحٰتِ اُولٰٓئِكَ هُمْ خَيْرُ الْبَرِيَّةِ ۝

جَزَآؤُهُمْ عِنْدَ رَبِّهِمْ جَنّٰتُ عَدْنٍ تَجْرِيْ مِنْ تَحْتِهَا الْاَنْهٰرُ خٰلِدِيْنَ فِيْهَا اَبَدًا ۗ رَضِيَ اللّٰهُ عَنْهُمْ وَرَضُوْا عَنْهُ ۗ ذٰلِكَ لِمَنْ خَشِيَ رَبَّهٗ ۝

Surah 98 Transliteration

Bismillahir Rahmanir Rahim

1. Lam yakunil ladheena kafaroo min ahlal kitaabe wal mushrekeena munfak keena hattaa ta-teyahoom ul bayyinah.

2. Rasoolun min Allahi yatloo suhufaan mutah harah.

3. Feehaa kutubun qayyimah.

4. Wa maa tafarraqal ladheena ootool kitaaba illaa min ba'de maa jaa-at humul bayyinah.

5. Wa maa oomiroo illaa leya'budool laha mukhliseena lahud deena hunafa-a wa yuqeemoos sawlaata wa yu-tuz zakaata wa dhaalika deenul qayyimah.

6. Innal ladheena kafaroo min ahlal kitaabi wal mushrekeena fee naari jahannama khawlideena feehaa, oola-eka hoom sharrul bariyyah.

7. Innal ladheena aamanu wa 'amiloos sawlihaati oola-eka hoom khaiyrul bariyyah.

8. Jazaa-u hoom 'inda rabbihim jannaatu 'adnin tajree min tahte haal anhaaru. Khawledeena feehaa abada. Radiyal lahu 'anhoom wa radoo 'anhu. Dhaalika leman khawshiya rabbah.

The Quaking
99 Al Zilzāl
Period Uncertain

*In the Name of Allah,
the Compassionate, the Merciful*

When the earth is shaken as deep as it can be shaken and when it throws out everything *buried in it,*

When people say in fear, *"What's happening to the earth?"* - that will be the day when the earth will show *its secrets* * by the order of its Lord. [1-5]

165

On that day, people will come forward in sorted groups to be shown the full account of their deeds. [6]

Whoever did a speck of good will see it, and whoever did a speck of evil will see it. [7-8]

💭 Think About It

When a man named Abu Sa'id al-Khudri heard the verses of this chapter, he asked the Prophet, "Do I have to watch all my deeds?"

The Prophet said, "Yes."

Then Abu Sa'id asked, "And all the big deeds?"

The Prophet again said, "Yes."

"And all the little deeds, too?" Abu Sa'id asked.

Then the Prophet said, "Yes," once more.

"Then I'm doomed!" Abu Sa'id cried out.

"Be happy, Abu Sa'id," the Prophet said, "because good deeds will be rewarded from ten to seven hundred times each, or even more if Allah wills, while bad deeds are counted only as one, or Allah just might forgive them altogether. Listen, no one will (go to Heaven) because of his actions alone."

"Not even you - the Messenger of Allah?" Abu Sa'id asked.

"No, not even me," the Prophet replied. "(Even I won't go to Heaven) unless Allah showers me with His mercy and favor." *(Bukhari, Muslim)*

----

1. How does this *hadith* relate to the message of this chapter?

2. Write a short story that focuses on the ideas in this *hadith*. (Allah counts true faith even more than good deeds.) You may also draw a picture that shows something that is mentioned in this chapter instead.

بِسْمِ اللهِ الرَّحْمٰنِ الرَّحِيْمِ

إِذَا زُلْزِلَتِ الْأَرْضُ زِلْزَالَهَا ۱

وَأَخْرَجَتِ الْأَرْضُ أَثْقَالَهَا ۲

وَقَالَ الْإِنْسَانُ مَا لَهَا ۳

يَوْمَئِذٍ تُحَدِّثُ أَخْبَارَهَا ۴

بِأَنَّ رَبَّكَ أَوْحٰى لَهَا ۵

يَوْمَئِذٍ يَّصْدُرُ النَّاسُ أَشْتَاتًا لِّيُرَوْا أَعْمَالَهُمْ ۶

فَمَنْ يَّعْمَلْ مِثْقَالَ ذَرَّةٍ خَيْرًا يَّرَهُ ۷

وَمَنْ يَّعْمَلْ مِثْقَالَ ذَرَّةٍ شَرًّا يَّرَهُ ۸

Surah 99 Transliteration

Bismillahir Rahmanir Rahim

1. Edhaa zul zilatil -ardu zil zaalahaa.

2. Wa akhra jatil -ardu ath qawlahaa.

3. Wa qawlal insaanu maa lahaa?

4. Yowma -edhin tuhad dithu akhbaarahaa.

5. Be anna rabbaka owhaalahaa.

6. Yowma -edhin yasdurun naasu ashtaatal leyurow 'amaalahoom.

7. Fa maiy ya'mal mithqawla dharratin khaiyraiy yarah.

8. Wa maiy ya'mal mithqawla dharratin sharraiy rah.

The Running Stallions

100 Al 'Ādiyāt
Early Meccan Period

Q BACKGROUND

People always want more and more stuff. When they go into stores, they rush at the shelves and want to buy everything. Have you ever felt like you had to just buy, buy, buy? It is a powerful feeling, indeed!

In this chapter, Allah uses the example of a charge of horses in a battle to show just how greedy people can be. In the next life, all the things we got here in this world won't matter at all. Allah is watching to see if we are greedy with our things or if we are sharing with others.

The Prophet said, "Whoever focuses only on the world (and its wealth), then Allah will make his life disorganized, and he will always think he is poor. He won't get from the world any more than what's been assigned for him.

"Whoever focuses his attention on the next life," the Prophet continued, "then his life will be organized for him, and his real wealth will be placed in his heart. The (wealth) of the world will then come to him anyway, (even though he doesn't try hard for it)." *(Ibn Majah)*

In the Name of Allah,
the Compassionate, the Merciful

Just like charging horses, running out of breath, making sparks fly up *with their hooves*, attacking at dawn, raising dust, racing forward, into the battle, storming on! [1-5]

170

People are thankless of their Lord, and, oh, how well they show it!

Their love for worldly wealth is real, and, oh, how strong they want it! [6-8]

Don't they know that when the graves are empty and when *all their secrets are revealed* - that on that day their Lord will know about them *and their greed*? [9-11]

 Think About It

1. Zaki wants a new toy every week. He is always bothering his parents and crying for more and more. When he gets a new toy, he throws it aside and asks for another one. What can you tell Zaki to help him change his ways?

2. How do people show that they are greedy? What do they do? What do they act like?

3. How does Allah use verses 1-5 to help us understand the strength and power of human greed?

بِسْمِ اللهِ الرَّحْمٰنِ الرَّحِيمِ

وَالْعٰدِيٰتِ ضَبْحًا ۞

فَالْمُورِيٰتِ قَدْحًا ۞

فَالْمُغِيرٰتِ صُبْحًا ۞

فَأَثَرْنَ بِهٖ نَقْعًا ۞

فَوَسَطْنَ بِهٖ جَمْعًا ۞

إِنَّ الْإِنْسَانَ لِرَبِّهٖ لَكَنُودٌ ۞

وَ إِنَّهٗ عَلٰى ذٰلِكَ لَشَهِيدٌ ۞

وَ إِنَّهٗ لِحُبِّ الْخَيْرِ لَشَدِيدٌ ۞

أَفَلَا يَعْلَمُ إِذَا بُعْثِرَ مَا فِى الْقُبُورِ ۞

وَحُصِّلَ مَا فِى الصُّدُورِ ۞

إِنَّ رَبَّهُمْ بِهِمْ يَوْمَئِذٍ لَّخَبِيرٌ ۞

Surah 100 Transliteration

Bismillahir Rahmanir Rahim

1. Wal 'aadeyaati dab haan.

2. Fal mureyaati qad haan.

3. Fal mugheeraati sub haan.

4. Fa atharna behe naq 'aan.

5. Fa wasatna behe jam 'aan.

6. Innal insaana le rabbihe la kanood.

7. Wa innahoo 'alaa dhaalika la shaheed.

8. Wa innahoo le hubbil khaiyri la shadeed.

9. Afalaa ya'lamu edhaa bu'thira maa fil quboor.

10. Wa hoossila maa fis sudoor.

11. Inna rabbahoom behim yowma -edhil la khabeer?

The Sudden Disaster
101 Al Qāri'ah
Early Meccan Period

🔍 BACKGROUND

The people of Mecca never believed that the world could end one day. They didn't even believe that human souls lived on after death. Allah makes the promise that He will end the world one day, even if people do not believe it.

*In the Name of Allah,
the Compassionate, the Merciful*

The sudden disaster! What's the sudden disaster, and how can you understand what the sudden disaster will be like? [1-3]

It's the day when people will look like moths fluttering *all over the place*, when the mountains will look like tangled hairballs blowing around. [4-5]

Then, whoever has more good deeds on his scale, he will be happy. [6-7]

While the one who has very few *good deeds* on his scale - the fire-pit will be like a mother to him, and how can you understand what the fire-pit is? It's like a hot, burning fire. [8-11]

☁️ Think About It

1. Why do you think that people who do more bad deeds than good should be punished?

2. Draw a picture based on verses 4-5 or verses 6-11. Give your drawing a title and show your friends as you read this chapter to them.

بِسْمِ اللهِ الرَّحْمٰنِ الرَّحِيمِ

الْقَارِعَةُ ۝

مَا الْقَارِعَةُ ۝

وَمَا أَدْرَاكَ مَا الْقَارِعَةُ ۝

يَوْمَ يَكُونُ النَّاسُ كَالْفَرَاشِ الْمَبْثُوثِ ۝

وَتَكُونُ الْجِبَالُ كَالْعِهْنِ الْمَنْفُوشِ ۝

فَأَمَّا مَنْ ثَقُلَتْ مَوَازِينُهُ ۝

فَهُوَ فِي عِيشَةٍ رَّاضِيَةٍ ۝

وَأَمَّا مَنْ خَفَّتْ مَوَازِينُهُ ۝

فَأُمُّهُ هَاوِيَةٌ ۝

وَمَا أَدْرَاكَ مَا هِيَهْ ۝

نَارٌ حَامِيَةٌ ۝

Surah 101 Transliteration

Bismillahir Rahmanir Rahim

1. Al Qaari'ah

2. Maal Qaari'ah?

3. Wa maa ad raaka maal Qaari'ah?

4. Yowma yakoonun naasu kaal faraashil mab thooth.

5. Wa takoonul jibaalu kaal 'ih nil manfoosh.

6. Fa ammaa man thaqulat mawaazeenuh.

7. Fa huwa fee 'ishatir raadiyah.

8. Wa ammaa man khaffat mawaazeenuh.

9. Fa oommuhu haawiyah.

10. Wa maa ad raaka maa hiyah?

11. Naarun haamiyah.

The Race (for Riches)

102 At-Takāthoor
Early Meccan Period

Q BACKGROUND

This chapter was revealed to the Prophet after he saw people from two different tribes in Mecca having a shouting match. Each tribe said that it was better and richer than the other. After he received this chapter from Angel Jibrael, the Prophet said that the message of this *surah* was so important that it was worth as much as a thousand other verses. *(Hakim, Bayhaqi)*

The Prophet also said, ""If the Son of Adam has a valley full of gold, he would want to have two valleys of gold, because nothing but the dirt of his grave will ever make his mouth full. Allah accepts the repentance of those who turn to Him and say they are sorry." *(Bukhari)*

In the Name of Allah,
the Compassionate, the Merciful

The endless race for money distracts you - *even 'til you go down to the grave.*

Oh, but you'll soon know *the foolishness of your goals*! And then again, oh yes, in time, you'll soon know! [1-4]

If you knew for sure *what lies ahead*, you would see Hellfire all around you, even as you'll no doubt see it clearly on a day when you'll be asked about *what you did with life's* opportunities. [5-8]

☁ Think About It

1. A man named 'Abdullah ibn Shikhir visited the Prophet one day, and he found the Prophet reciting this chapter. After he finished reciting it, the Prophet turned to him and said:

"The son of Adam says, 'This is my money. This is my property,' but you get nothing from your things except for what you eat and use up, the clothes you wear and then wear out, and the money you give away in charity and so gain (as an investment in the next life). Everything else besides these things will pass away, and other people will inherit them." (Muslim)

What is the main lesson of this hadith and how does this chapter of the Qur'an (chapter 102) support that idea?

2. How do verses 1-4 try to convinve us that we should focus our lives on more than just money?

3. Why is it a foolish goal to only live for money?

4. According to the background story of this chapter, what is the only thing that can ever satisfy the greediness of people?

بِسْمِ اللهِ الرَّحْمٰنِ الرَّحِيْمِ

اَلْهٰىكُمُ التَّكَاثُرُ ۟ ١

حَتّٰى زُرْتُمُ الْمَقَابِرَ ۟ ٢

كَلَّا سَوْفَ تَعْلَمُوْنَ ۟ ٣

ثُمَّ كَلَّا سَوْفَ تَعْلَمُوْنَ ۟ ٤

كَلَّا لَوْ تَعْلَمُوْنَ عِلْمَ الْيَقِيْنِ ۟ ٥

لَتَرَوُنَّ الْجَحِيْمَ ۟ ٦

ثُمَّ لَتَرَوُنَّهَا عَيْنَ الْيَقِيْنِ ۟ ٧

ثُمَّ لَتُسْئَلُنَّ يَوْمَئِذٍ عَنِ النَّعِيْمِ ۟ ٨

Surah 102 Transliteration

Bismillahir Rahmanir Rahim

1. Al haakumut ta kaathur.

2. Hattaa zurtumul maqawbir.

3. Kallaa sowfa ta'lamoon.

4. Thoomma kallaa sowfa ta'lamoon.

5. Kallaa louw ta'lamoona 'ilmal yaqeen.

6. La tara oonnal jaheem.

7. Thoomma la tara oonahaa 'aiynal yaqeen.

8. Thoomma la tus-aloonna yowma -edhin 'anin na'eem.

The Passage of Time
103 Al 'Asr
Early Meccan Period

⌕ BACKGROUND

This chapter is very short, but the lesson is huge. It is about how time passes and history changes. What do people learn from the past? Does learning about the past make them better? Think of all the people and time periods that you've learned about in your social studies classes. Who were the good people and who were the bad? Who made mistakes and who got hurt? What always happened to the bad people in the end?

The evil people always lose and they get destroyed in one way or another. Nobody remembers them with kind words and they do nothing good in the world. Who would want to be remembered as an evil, horrible person? On the other hand, the good people who are afraid of making Allah angry with them are the ones we remember and celebrate. If people paid attention to this lesson, they would try hard not to be bad.

This chapter was so important to the companions of the Prophet that they would often say it at the end of meetings to remind themselves that they are only a small moment in history. This helped them to focus on the good things. (Tabarani)

*In the Name of Allah,
the Compassionate, the Merciful*

The lessons of history *are the proof* that people are always losing - all except *for the people* who believe in Allah and do what's right and who also teach each other to be truthful and patient *with hardships*. [1-3]

☁ Think About It

1. Choose one topic from your social studies class that shows how people were being bad to others and then were destroyed or taken over by others, and explain how this chapter can relate to that event. Did those people live forever? Who took them over? Who were the good people whose names we remember? Who were the bad people from those days? You can write your answer, or draw a picture here that shows what happened.

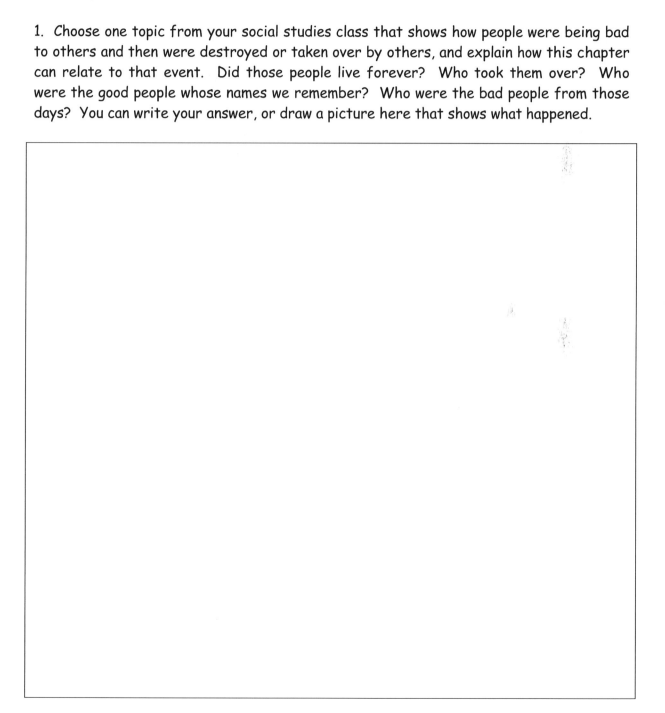

بِسْمِ اللهِ الرَّحْمٰنِ الرَّحِيمِ

وَالْعَصْرِ ۝

إِنَّ الْإِنْسَانَ لَفِي خُسْرٍ ۝

إِلَّا الَّذِينَ آمَنُوا وَعَمِلُوا الصّٰلِحٰتِ

وَتَوَاصَوْا بِالْحَقِّ ۝ وَتَوَاصَوْا بِالصَّبْرِ ۝

Surah 103 Transliteration

Bismillahir Rahmanir Rahim

1. Wal 'Asr.

2. Innal insaana lafee khusr.

3. Illal ladheena aamanoo wa 'amilus sawlihaati wa tawaasow bil haqqi wa tawaasow bis sabr.

The Slanderer
104 Al Humazah
Early Meccan Period

🔍 BACKGROUND

There was a very bad man named Akhnas ibn Shariq. He lived in Mecca and used to worship idols. When the Prophet started teaching people about Islam, Akhnas started teasing him and saying bad things about him to other people. Talking bad about others and calling them bad names is a sin in Islam. This chapter warns people not to do that.

A man once asked the Prophet to explain to him what kind of talking behind someone's back was bad. The Prophet replied, "It is saying something about your brother (in faith) that he would not like you to say." The man then asked, "What if (the bad thing) that I said about my brother was true?" The Prophet answered, "If what you said about him was true, then you still would have been doing backbiting, and if what you said about him was false, then you would have lied against him." (Abu Dawud, Tirmidhi)

In the Name of Allah,
the Compassionate, the Merciful

A warning to every name caller and backbiter who saves his money for the future. Is he hoping to buy a life that never ends? [1-3]

No way! He'll be thrown into the `Crusher`, and how can you understand what the `Crusher` is? [4-5]

It's the anger of Allah built up into a huge fire.

It will go all the way through them * and *cover them under endless pillars.* [6-9]

How do you think it would feel to go in a place like you see in the picture above?

Who can save you from that horrible place?

Write the word 'CRUSHER' in a really cool and artistic way on the line below.

_____

Think About It

1. Amirah and Zakiyyah were best friends. One day they got into an argument over a bracelet that they found on the floor. Amirah wanted to keep it and Zakiyyah wanted to give it to the teacher. Later that day, Zakiyyah saw Amirah talking badly about her to a group of girls in the hall. If you were a good Muslim like Zakiyyah, what would you do and why?

2. The introduction to the chapter had some advice from the Prophet. The man had asked him if we can say bad things about others if the bad things are true. What did the Prophet tell him?

3. Why is talking behind people's backs so harmful to both the person doing the gossiping and the one who is the victim?

بِسْمِ اللهِ الرَّحْمٰنِ الرَّحِيْمِ

وَيْلٌ لِّكُلِّ هُمَزَةٍ لُّمَزَةِۙ ۝١

الَّذِىْ جَمَعَ مَالًا وَّعَدَّدَهٗۙ ۝٢

يَحْسَبُ اَنَّ مَالَهٗۤ اَخْلَدَهٗ ۝٣

كَلَّا لَيُنۢبَذَنَّ فِى الْحُطَمَةِ ۝٤

وَمَاۤ اَدْرٰىكَ مَا الْحُطَمَةُ ۝٥

نَارُ اللهِ الْمُوْقَدَةُۙ ۝٦

الَّتِىْ تَطَّلِعُ عَلَى الْاَفْـِٕدَةِ ۝٧

اِنَّهَا عَلَيْهِمْ مُّؤْصَدَةٌۙ ۝٨

فِىْ عَمَدٍ مُّمَدَّدَةٍ ۝٩

Surah 104 Transliteration

Bismillahir Rahmanir Rahim

1. Waiy lulli koolle humazatil lumazah.

2. Alladhee jama'a maalaaw wa 'ad dadah.

3. Yah sabu anna maalahu akhladah.

4. Kallaa layoom badhanna fil hutamah.

5. Wa maa ad raaka maal hutamah?

6. Naarul lahil mooqadah.

7. Allatee tat tale'oo 'alaal af-idah.

8. Innahaa 'alayhim mu-sawdah.

9. Fee amadin mumad dadah.

The Elephant

105 Al Feel
Early Meccan Period

Q BACKGROUND

Arabia was a land of many different religions. In the south there was a Christian-ruled land named Yemen. In the year just before the Prophet was born, Abrahah, the king of Yemen became jealous of the Ka'bah of Mecca. All the Arabs went there to worship their idols and spend their money. Abrahah built a huge church to attract the Arabs, but they were not interested.

One Arab visitor to the church even insulted the building by going to the bathroom on a wall! Abrahah got mad and marched an army to Mecca to destroy the Ka'bah. He brought along some big elephants to knock it down. The Meccans were afraid and ran to hide in the hills when the army came near. They said that Allah should defend the Ka'bah, because they would not do it.

Then a miracle happened. The elephants refused to enter Mecca, and a then a strange disaster fell upon the army of Abrahah while they were waiting in their camp. The soldiers were plagued with big sores and they started dying.

Some said that birds dropped stones on them, while others said it was flying bugs that spread diseases. Abrahah was scared and he ran all the way back to Yemen, but he also died of the disease soon after returning. Allah defended His holy building!

In the Name of Allah,
the Compassionate, the Merciful

Haven't you seen how your Lord stopped the army of the elephant? Didn't He stop their evil plans? [1-2]

He let loose upon them a swarm of flying things that struck them down with stone-smacked sores. [3-4]

In the end, *the soldiers* looked like they were cut down crops in the field. [5]

191

Write down what you think the men are saying:

Man #1:

Man #2

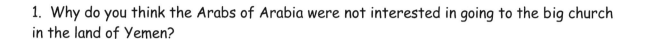

Think About It

1. Why do you think the Arabs of Arabia were not interested in going to the big church in the land of Yemen?

2. Why do you think the elephants did not want to destroy the Ka'bah?

3. Some people say it was birds dropping stones on the soldiers. Others say it was flying bugs that bit them and spread diseases. In any case, why do you think Allah stopped this army and destroyed its fighting power?

بِسْمِ اللّٰهِ الرَّحْمٰنِ الرَّحِيْمِ

اَلَمْ تَرَ كَيْفَ فَعَلَ رَبُّكَ بِاَصْحٰبِ الْفِيْلِ ۝١

اَلَمْ يَجْعَلْ كَيْدَهُمْ فِيْ تَضْلِيْلٍ ۝٢

وَّاَرْسَلَ عَلَيْهِمْ طَيْرًا اَبَابِيْلَ ۝٣

تَرْمِيْهِمْ بِحِجَارَةٍ مِّنْ سِجِّيْلٍ ۝٤

فَجَعَلَهُمْ كَعَصْفٍ مَّأْكُوْلٍ ۝٥

Surah 105 Transliteration

Bismillahir Rahmanir Rahim

1. A lam tara kaiyfa fa'ala rabbuka be as haabil feel?

2. A lam yaj 'al kaiyda hoom fee tad leel?

3. Wa arsala 'alayhim taiyran abaabeel.

4. Tarmeehim be hijaaratim min sijjeel.

5. Fa ja 'alahoom ka 'asfin ma-kool.

The Quraysh
106 Quraysh
Early Meccan Period

🔍 BACKGROUND

This chapter is about the tribe of Quraysh. The Quraysh were a large group of related families that controlled the city of Mecca. They got very rich from two things. The first way was from the fact that the Ka'bah was under their control. The Arab tribes of the desert all brought their idols to the Ka'bah and would visit them (and spend money) all the time.

The second way the Quraysh got rich was through trade. They would organize huge caravans to travel north to Syria in the summer and south to Yemen in the winter. They made trade agreements with many tribes along the way.

The Quraysh thought all this good fortune was by their own hands. They used to say they got all their food from their own planning, even though they lived in the desert. In this chapter, Allah is reminding them that He owns the Ka'bah and that He brings the food to them and keeps them safe on their journeys.

In the Name of Allah,
the Compassionate, the Merciful

Now about the treaties that the Quraysh made *to travel safely through other lands*, those treaties that protect them on their journeys through winter and summer: [1-2]

They should serve the Lord of this House (the Ka'bah) *instead of their false idols*, because *Allah* is the One Who gives them their food so they're not hungry, and *He's the One Who* keeps them safe *so they don't have to feel* afraid. [3-4]

196

🗯 Think About It

1. Think of a time when you were traveling with your family. What are two things that *could* have gone wrong on your trip but didn't happen?

2. Why was it wrong for the Quraysh to worship idols instead of Allah?

3. The Prophet said, "Allah has given seven advantages to the Quraysh that He didn't give to anyone else (among the Arabs): I am from them, prophethood was instituted among them (over all other Arab tribes), they're the custodians of the Ka'bah, they offer the water of Zamzam, Allah helped them to overcome the Army of the Elephant, they alone had people worshipping Allah for ten years before anyone else (had accepted Islam), and Allah revealed this chapter about them." Then the Prophet recited this chapter. *(Bayhaqi)*

What is one advantage of the Quraysh that is being talked about in this hadeeth?

بِسْمِ اللهِ الرَّحْمٰنِ الرَّحِيمِ

لِإِيلٰفِ قُرَيْشٍ ۝١

إِۦلٰفِهِمْ رِحْلَةَ الشِّتَاءِ وَالصَّيْفِ ۝٢

فَلْيَعْبُدُوا رَبَّ هٰذَا الْبَيْتِ ۝٣

الَّذِيٓ أَطْعَمَهُمْ مِّنْ جُوعٍ ۝ ۵

وَّءَامَنَهُمْ مِّنْ خَوْفٍ ۝٤

Surah 106 Transliteration

Bismillahir Rahmanir Rahim

1. Lee eelaafe Quraysh,

2. Eelaa feehim reh la tash sheetaa-e was saiyf.

3. Fal ya'abudoo rabba hadhal bayt.

4. Alladhee at'amahoom min joo'in wa aamana hoom min khowf.

Small Favors
107 Al Mā'ūn
Early Meccan Period

🔍 BACKGROUND

One day, Abu Sufyan, an important chief of the Quraysh tribe, was preparing two lambs for dinner. An orphan came and asked him for some food, and Abu Sufyan became angry and hit him. The orphan ran away crying. This chapter was revealed to the Prophet to answer the mean actions of people who feel they don't have to help poor people.

It also warns us that even people who pray a lot and seem to be religious can be mean in their hearts. Allah does not love people who are hypocrites like that. One way to test your faith and to know if you are really a good believer is to think about how you react to those who are weaker or poorer than you. If you want to be kind to the people and animals around you, then your faith has a solid foundation to grow upon! Practice being kind and Allah will love and reward you for your goodness.

In the Name of Allah,
the Compassionate, the Merciful

Have you seen the person who denies the *good* way of life? He pushes the orphans aside and doesn't want to feed the poor. [1-3]

So this is a warning to people who pray but who are careless in their worship, whose prayers are only for show, and yet who don't want to share even the smallest of favors. [4-7]

☁ Think About It

1. How is being cruel or mean a sign that your understanding of religion is all wrong?

2. If you were a poor person on the side of the road, and then you saw someone walking by with shopping bags full of food, how would you feel and why? What would you say to the person who had the food?

3. Using the opposite of the things mentioned in this chapter, how can a person show they are good and true in their religion?

بِسْمِ اللهِ الرَّحْمٰنِ الرَّحِيْمِ

اَرَءَيْتَ الَّذِىْ يُكَذِّبُ بِالدِّيْنِ ۚ ۝١

فَذٰلِكَ الَّذِىْ يَدُعُّ الْيَتِيْمَ ۙ ۝٢

وَلَا يَحُضُّ عَلٰى طَعَامِ الْمِسْكِيْنِ ۚ ۝٣

فَوَيْلٌ لِّلْمُصَلِّيْنَ ۙ ۝٤

الَّذِيْنَ هُمْ عَنْ صَلَاتِهِمْ سَاهُوْنَ ۙ ۝٥

الَّذِيْنَ هُمْ يُرَآءُوْنَ ۙ ۝٦

وَيَمْنَعُوْنَ الْمَاعُوْنَ ۝٧

Surah 107 Transliteration

Bismillahir Rahmanir Rahim

1. Ara aiyt alladhee yukadh dhebu bid deen?

2. Fa dhaalikal ladhee yadu' ul yateem.

3. Wa laa yahud du 'alaa ta'aamil miskeen.

4. Fa waiylul lil musalleen.

5. Alladheena hoom 'an sawlatehim saahoon.

6. Alladheena hoom yuraa-un.

7. Wa yamna 'oonal ma'oon.

Abundance
108 Al Kawthar
Early Meccan Period

🔍 BACKGROUND

The Prophet's wife Khadijah had given birth to a baby boy named 'Abdullah. Sadly, he died a short time later. Muhammad was very heartbroken, and then a very mean idol-worshipper named Al 'As ibn Wa'il came and started making fun of him about that. Ibn Wa'il often said of Muhammad, "Leave him be; he has no sons, and no one will remember his name after he dies."

Abu Lahab, a very mean uncle of the Prophet, also started to tease the Prophet about having no sons. A few days later, the Prophet was sitting with some of his companions, and he looked sleepy. After a while he lifted his head, smiled and said, "A chapter has been revealed to me."

Then after reciting this chapter, he asked, "Do you know what abundance (*kawthar*) is?" "Allah and His Messenger know best," they replied.

Then the Prophet said, "It's a river in Paradise, filled with blessings. It's been given to me by Allah. On the Day of Judgment, my people will gather around it, and it will fill as many cups as there are stars in the sky. Some people will be pushed away from it, and I'm going to ask, 'But my Lord! They're also my followers!' Then a voice will say, '(No, not really) because you don't know what happened after you.'" *(Ahmad)*

In the Name of Allah,
the Compassionate, the Merciful

(Muhammad,) We have given you so many *gifts*, so now turn to your Lord in prayer and sacrifice. [1-2]

For sure, it will be the ones who insult *you* who will have *their future* cut off. [3]

💭 Think About It

1. Why do you think Allah will give the Prophet a special river in Paradise?

2. If you saw someone teasing another person because someone special died, what could you say to the bad person to get them to stop and to be respectful?

بِسْمِ اللهِ الرَّحْمٰنِ الرَّحِيْمِ

اِنَّآ اَعْطَيْنٰكَ الْكَوْثَرَ ۞

فَصَلِّ لِرَبِّكَ وَانْحَرْ ۞

اِنَّ شَانِئَكَ هُوَ الْاَبْتَرُ ۞

Surah 108 Transliteration

Bismillahir Rahmanir Rahim

1. Innaa 'ataiynaa kal kowthar.

2. Fasalle le rabbika wan har.

3. Inna shaa ne-aka hoowal abtar.

The Faithless

109 Al Kāfiroon
Early Meccan Period

🔍 BACKGROUND

The idol-worshippers of Mecca thought they could protect their religion if they got Muhammad to make a deal with them. Some leaders of the Quraysh told Muhammad that if he worshipped their gods for a year, then they would worship his One God for a year.

After that, they would talk about whose religion was better. Muhammad did not accept their offer. When they said, "At least touch some of our gods (in respect), and then we'll believe in you," Allah revealed this chapter to the Prophet, and he said it to them. (Qurtubi)

In the Name of Allah,
the Compassionate, the Merciful

Say (to them): "Hey, all you who hide faith in Allah! I don't serve what you serve, and you don't serve what I do." [1-3]

"And I won't serve what you serve, nor will you serve what I do. To you, your way of life, and to me, mine." [4-6]

Think About It

1. Why do you think the idol-worshippers wanted to make a deal with the Prophet?

2. Read the verses taken from chapter 19 below. This is the story of Abraham and his father. His father was an idol worshipper.

Abraham and His Father

Mention in the Book (something about) Abraham, because he was an honest man and a prophet. * He said to his father, *"My father! Why are you worshipping things that can not hear nor see nor bring you any benefit at all? * My father! Some teachings have come to me that have not reached you, so follow me, and I will guide you to a correct path."* [41-43]

*"My father! Don't be in the service of Shaytan, for Shaytan is a rebel against the Compassionate. * My father! I'm afraid that a punishment might befall you from the Compassionate that may cause you to be included among Shaytan's allies."* [44-45]

"Are you talking against my gods?" (his father) demanded. *"Abraham! If you don't back off, then I'll stone you! Now get yourself away from me!"* [46]

"So peace (and good bye) to you then." (Abraham) answered. *"However, I'm still going to pray to my Lord for your forgiveness, because He has always been kind to me."* [47]

"Now I'm going to turn away from you and from those whom you call upon besides Allah. All I can do is call upon my Lord and hope my prayer to my Lord doesn't go unanswered." [48]

And so he turned away from (his people) and from those (false gods) that they worshipped besides Allah. [49]

How are the messages from chapter 109 and from these verses above similar?

بِسْمِ اللّٰهِ الرَّحْمٰنِ الرَّحِيْمِ

قُلْ يٰٓاَيُّهَا الْكٰفِرُوْنَ ۙ ۱

لَآ اَعْبُدُ مَا تَعْبُدُوْنَ ۙ ۲

وَلَآ اَنْتُمْ عٰبِدُوْنَ مَآ اَعْبُدُ ۚ ۳

وَلَآ اَنَا عَابِدٌ مَّا عَبَدْتُّمْ ۙ ۴

وَلَآ اَنْتُمْ عٰبِدُوْنَ مَآ اَعْبُدُ ۗ ۵

لَكُمْ دِيْنُكُمْ وَلِيَ دِيْنِ ۶

Surah 109 Transliteration

Bismillahir Rahmanir Rahim

1. Qul yaa aiy yuhaal kaafiroon!

2. Laa 'abudu maa ta'budoon.

3. Wa laa antoom 'aabiduna maa 'abud.

4. Wa laa anaa 'aabidum maa 'abed toom.

5. Wa laa antoom 'aabidoona maa 'abud.

6. Lakoom deenukoom wa leeya deen.

The Help (of Allah)
110 An-Nasr
Late Medinan Period

🔍 BACKGROUND

This is the last chapter that was revealed to the Prophet. By this time, Islam was the religion of most of Arabia. It had been a long struggle and the people were happy to be Muslims.

After the Prophet recited this chapter, he said, "The people (of the world) are on one side, and me and my companions are on the other side. There is no more migration after the takeover (of Mecca). All that is left for Muslims to do is *jihad* (working hard in Allah's cause) and to have good intentions (about what they do)." (Tabarani)

In the Name of Allah,
the Compassionate, the Merciful

When the help of Allah comes to you and there is victory. [1]

When you see people rushing into Allah's way of life in big crowds. [2]

That is when you must glorify your Lord and ask Him for His forgiveness *so you can be reminded to be humble,* because He is the One Who listens when people say they are sorry. [3]

🗨 Think About It

1. After winning everything, why do you think that we should still remember that we need to always be humble towards Allah?

2. The word humble means to be extra nice to someone when you know they are better or more powerful than you. It also means that we do not act like we are super great in front of others. Verse 3 gives us a good reason why we should be humble to Allah? What is the reason?

بِسْمِ اللهِ الرَّحْمَنِ الرَّحِيمِ

إِذَا جَاءَ نَصْرُ اللهِ وَالْفَتْحُ ۝

وَرَأَيْتَ النَّاسَ يَدْخُلُونَ فِي دِينِ اللهِ أَفْوَاجًا ۝

فَسَبِّحْ بِحَمْدِ رَبِّكَ وَاسْتَغْفِرْهُ إِنَّهُ كَانَ تَوَّابًا ۝

214

Surah 110 Transliteration

Bismillahir Rahmanir Rahim

1. Edhaa jaa-a nasrullahi wal fet-hu.

2. Wa ra aiytan naasa yed khuloona fee deen illahe afwaja.

3. Fasab bih be hamdi rabbika wa staghfirhu. Innahu kaana tawwaba.

Flame
111 Lahab
Early Meccan Period

🔍 BACKGROUND

After three years of teaching in secret, Allah commanded the Prophet to tell everyone about Islam. So he stood on a small hill and started shouting for people to come to him. Everyone came and the Prophet said, "(People of Quraysh)! If I told you that an army was coming on the other side of this hill, would you believe me?"

Someone in the crowd said, "Yes, because we've never heard you tell a lie." Then Muhammad said, "So now I'm warning you about of a big punishment (if you don't give up your idols and believe in Allah)!" A rude uncle of the Prophet named Abu Lahab got angry, and he said, "You gathered us here just for *this*? May you be cut off!" Then Abu Lahab threw a rock at him. *(Bukhari)*

Abu Lahab's wife Urwa was already talking bad about Muhammad before this. Now she said she would sell her necklace to have money to use against Islam. After she heard about this chapter, she came out looking for Muhammad with a sharp stone in her hand to hurt him. Muhammad was sitting with his friend Abu Bakr, and she came near to them. She did not notice the Prophet and instead talked in a rude way to Abu Bakr. Then she left. Allah protected the Prophet from Urwa and Abu Lahab. *(Ibn Kathir)*

*In the Name of Allah,
the Compassionate, the Merciful*

Cut off are *the works* of Abu Lahab's hands - cut off! Neither his money nor what he has completed *in this world* will save him, for he will soon be in a big fire. And his woman, who will be made to feed the flames, will have around her neck a twisted fiber chain. [1-5]

🗨 Think About It

1. Why did the people say they would believe the Prophet if he said an army was coming?

2. What does the twisted fiber chain have to do with Urwah and what she did in this world? (Hint: what jewelry did she have in the world that she used for evil?)

بِسْمِ اللهِ الرَّحْمٰنِ الرَّحِيْمِ

تَبَّتْ يَدَآ أَبِيْ لَهَبٍ وَّتَبَّ ۝

مَآ أَغْنٰى عَنْهُ مَالُهُ وَمَا كَسَبَ ۝

سَيَصْلٰى نَارًا ذَاتَ لَهَبٍ ۝

وَّامْرَأَتُهُ ۚ حَمَّالَةَ الْحَطَبِ ۝

فِيْ جِيْدِهَا حَبْلٌ مِّنْ مَّسَدٍ ۝

Surah 111 Transliteration

Bismillahir Rahmanir Rahim

1. Tebbat yedaa abee lahabiw wa tebb.

2. Maa agh naa 'anhu maa luhu wa maa kasab.

3. Sayas laa naaron thaata lahab.

4. Wa am ra a tuhu hammaa latal hatawb.

5. Fee jeedehaa hablum mim masad.

Pure Faith
112 Al Ikhlās
Early Meccan Period

🔍 BACKGROUND

A group of visiting Jews asked Muhammad to describe what Allah was like. They wanted to compare his description of Allah with what their own holy books said. They asked him if his God was male or female, made of gold, copper or silver, whether He eats and drinks, how He came to be in control of the earth, and who will control it after Him.

The Prophet waited patiently for a few days for a revelation from Allah. Then the Prophet sent word to his followers to gather in front of his house and that he would recite one-third of the Qur'an for them. They gathered at the right time, and after the Prophet recited this short chapter to them, he went back in his house.

The people were confused because they thought they were going to hear one-third of the whole Qur'an, and some people thought that the Prophet was inside and receiving more revelations from Allah. The Prophet came out of his door again and said, "Listen, this chapter is equal to one-third of the Qur'an." *(Tirmidhi)*

In the Name of Allah,
the Compassionate, the Merciful

Say (to them): "He is only one God. Allah is Always and Forever." [1-2]

"He does not have any children and was He never born. There is nothing that is the same as Him." [3-4]

⚘ Think About It

1. Do you think that Muslims believe that Allah looks like a man, like the Jews and Christians believe? What is the proof?

2. Some people believe that God is three separate people that together make up one person. Other people say that God was born on earth one time or many times. A lot of people in the world make statues, paintings and drawings of what they say Allah looks like. How would you as a Muslim use this chapter to describe the differences in how we believe in God and how they believe in God?

بِسْمِ اللهِ الرَّحْمٰنِ الرَّحِيْمِ

قُلْ هُوَ اللهُ أَحَدٌ ۝١

اللهُ الصَّمَدُ ۝٢

لَمْ يَلِدْ ەۥ وَلَمْ يُوْلَدْ ۝٣

وَلَمْ يَكُنْ لَّهٗ كُفُوًا أَحَدٌ ۝٤

Surah 112 Transliteration

Bismillahir Rahmanir Rahim

1. Qul huwallahu ahad.

2. Allahus Sawmad.

3. Lem Yalid wa lem yulad.

4. Wa lem yakullahu kufuwan ahad.

Daybreak
113 Al Falaq
Period Uncertain

🔍 BACKGROUND

Prophet Muhammad started to feel strange one day. He couldn't remember if he did things or didn't do things. He thought that maybe someone put an evil magic spell on him to make him forgetful. A few days later, the Prophet had a dream. In that dream two people were talking about what happened to him. The two men then pointed to a small tree. When the Prophet woke up, he went out and looked for the tree that he saw in his dream. He found the tree.

There was an old dry well nearby, and in it he found a rock with a comb and a single hair wrapped around it. He also found a rope with a bunch of knots tied in it. A man named Labid had used that very same comb on the Prophet a few weeks before. Labid had used the piece of hair he took from the Prophet to cast an evil magic spell on him. The Prophet untied the knots in the rope and broke the comb and the hair. The spell was gone and the Prophet could think clearly again. His wife A'ishah asked him, "Won't you tell everyone about this?" He replied, "Allah has cured me, and I hate to spread talk of bad times to other people." *(Bukhari)*

In the Name of Allah,
the Compassionate, the Merciful

Say (out loud): "I want to be safe with the Lord of the Dawn from the evil dangers in the created world, from the evil of darkness when it comes, from the evil of people who cast magic spells and from the evil of people who give *me* mean looks when they're jealous." [1-5]

Think About It

1.   Think of a time when you felt scared or alone.   What helped you to feel better afterwards?

2.   What did Labid do to the Prophet that made the Prophet feel strange?

3.   What did the Prophet see in his dream?

4.   How did the Prophet break the evil spell?

بِسْمِ اللَّهِ الرَّحْمَٰنِ الرَّحِيمِ

قُلْ أَعُوذُ بِرَبِّ الْفَلَقِ ۝

مِنْ شَرِّ مَا خَلَقَ ۝

وَمِنْ شَرِّ غَاسِقٍ إِذَا وَقَبَ ۝

وَمِنْ شَرِّ النَّفَّاثَاتِ فِي الْعُقَدِ ۝

وَمِنْ شَرِّ حَاسِدٍ إِذَا حَسَدَ ۝

Surah 113 Transliteration

Bismillahir Rahmanir Rahim

1. Qul 'owdhoobe rabbil falaq.

2. Min sharri maa khalaq.

3. Wa min sharri ghawsiqin edhaa waqab.

4. Wa min sharrin naf faathaate fil 'uqad.

5. Wa min sharri haasidin edhaa hasad.

People
114 An-Nās
Period Uncertain

🔍 BACKGROUND

The Shaytan and his followers are always trying to scare us and make us do the wrong things. Sometimes we feel a bad thought and our brain seems to order us to do a bad deed. This might be the whispers of Shaytan's army of evil jinns. Other times a friend might tell us to do something bad.

We must fight the whispers that tell us to do bad deeds, no matter where they come from! The Prophet said: "Shaytan is waiting there above the heart of the son of Adam. When (the person) forgets about Allah, Shaytan whispers to him (to do bad deeds). When the person remembers Allah again, then Shaytan moves back." *(at-Tabari)*

In the Name of Allah,
the Compassionate, the Merciful

Say (out loud): "I want to be safe with the Lord of people, the King of people, the God of people, from the little thoughts of evil, whispered into the hearts of people by jinns or other people." [1-6]

Think About It

1. The Prophet once said:

   "Shaytan puts his hand on a person's heart. If he finds it filled with good words for Allah, he takes his hand away. If he finds that the person's heart is forgetful of Allah, then he takes over the person's heart completely, and this is the whispering of the jinns." *(Musnad Abu Ya'la)*

   How does the saying of the Prophet relate to the message of this surah?

2. The Prophet said that when we say, "Aoodhu billa himina shaytanir rajeem" that this makes the Shaytan go away. It means, "Allah protect me from the bad Shaytan." Pretend that you feel bad thoughts coming into your brain. Say this sentence to make Shaytan go away!

   How can you fill your heart with good words for Allah?

   By doing something called *dhikr*. That is to say good words about Allah over and over. One common *dhikr* phrase is, "*Subhanullah wa behamdihi.*"

   This means, "Glory to Allah and all good words are for Him." Learn it and say it often. If you say it 100 times you get all your small sins forgiven!

229

بِسْمِ اللَّهِ الرَّحْمَٰنِ الرَّحِيمِ

قُلْ أَعُوذُ بِرَبِّ النَّاسِ ۝

مَلِكِ النَّاسِ ۝

إِلَٰهِ النَّاسِ ۝

مِن شَرِّ الْوَسْوَاسِ ۞ الْخَنَّاسِ ۝

الَّذِي يُوَسْوِسُ فِي صُدُورِ النَّاسِ ۝

مِنَ الْجِنَّةِ وَالنَّاسِ ۝

Bismillahir Rahmanir Rahim

1. Qul 'owdhoobee Rabbin Naas.

2. Malikin Naas.

3. Eelahin Naas.

4. Min sharril waswaa sil khan naas.

5. Alladhee yuwas wesu fee soodoor in naas.

6. Minal jinnati wan naas.

**Don't Forget
There are Other
Volumes in this
Learning Series of Books**

**See them at
www.amirahpublishing.com**

Selected Other Books for Kids by Yahiya Emerick

Visit: www.amirahpublishing.com to see the latest books!

Layla Deen and the Case of the Ramadan Rogue
By Yahiya Emerick

Somebody's trying to ruin her Ramadan! Layla Deen and her family were just settling in to break a long days fast when their mother came running from the kitchen and cried, "*Someone stole the food for Iftar!*" Layla knew it was a terrible crime and decided to get to the bottom of this mystery. See what happens! Illustrated. Ages 8-16.

Ahmad Deen and the Curse of the Aztec Warrior
By Yahiya Emerick

Where is he? Ahmad Deen and his sister Layla thought they were getting a nice vacation in tropical Mexico. But what they're really going to get is a hair-raising race against time to save their father from becoming the next victim of an ancient, bloody ritual! How can Ahmad save his father and deal with his bratty sister at the same time? To make matters worse, no one seems to want to help them find the mysterious lost city that may hold the key to their father's whereabouts. And then there's that jungle guide with the strangely familiar jacket. Are they brave enough—or crazy enough, to take on the Curse of the Aztec Warrior? Illustrated. Ages 8-16.

Ahmad Deen and the Jinn at Shaolin
By Yahiya Emerick

A once in a lifetime chance! Ahmad Deen is one of ten lucky students in his school who gets an all-expense paid trip to China. But instead of *getting* a history lesson, Ahmad may become a victim *of* history as he is thrust in the middle of a bizarre web of superstition, corruption and ancient hatreds that seek to destroy all who interfere. Who kidnapped his room-mate? What clue can only be found in the Shaolin Temple? How will Ahmad learn the Kung-Fu skills he'll need to defeat the powers of darkness. or will he fall prey to the mysterious *Jinn at Shaolin?* Illustrated. Ages 9-16.

Layla Deen and the Popularity Contest
By Yahiya Emerick

Layla is in junior high now, and she has found it hard to adjust. Friends seem in short supply so Layla becomes quiet and withdrawn. Then a school popularity contest throws her world into a tailspin. Find out what happens. Ages 9-16.

Isabella: A Girl of Muslim Spain
By Yahiya Emerick

A classic tale about a young girl who finds Islam, and danger, amidst the harrowing religious conflicts of medieval Muslim Spain. Experience firsthand what life was like in the splendid Muslim city of Cordoba. See through the eyes of Isabella as she struggles with her father's beliefs and finds that life is not always as easy as people think. Embark on a journey into history, into the heart, as you follow her path from darkness into light. Illustrated. Ages 10+

The Seafaring Beggar and Other Tales
By Yahiya Emerick

A delightful collection of short stories, poems, essays and other writings that showcase a variety of themes and inspirational nuggets of wisdom. Many of these stories and poems have been published in international magazines and are sure to put a smile on your face and a warmth in your heart for the beauty that is Islam. Illustrated. Ages 10+

Qur'an

The Meaning of the Holy Qur'an for School Children
Compiled by Yahiya Emerick

For the first time ever we now have a complete translation of the entire Qur'an into kid-friendly English. Complete with simple line drawings and background information – this is indispensable for the home and your children. For grades 4-7.

A Journey through the Holy Qur'an
Presented by Yahiya Emerick

An easy to read translation with the reasons for revelation interspersed throughout the text so that the Qur'an and its background can be better understood. Ages 14 - adult.

The Holy Qur'an in Today's English
Presented by Yahiya Emerick

This book contains the main text of the Qur'an with reasons for revelation at the bottom of each page in footnote format. It contains other commentary and resources, as well. Great for personal study and inspirational reading. Ages 16 - adult.

The Holy Qur'an: As If You Were There
Presented by Yahiya Emerick

This is a translation of the Holy Qur'an meant for teenagers. It has all the reasons for revelation that explain the background of the verses. It also has lots of thiking questions and great explanations for the menaing of different verses and concepts. Ages 12 - adult.

See more at:

www.amirahpublishing.com

237